YOU ARE GOD

It's Time to Shine

John McIntosh

It is important to be aware that to shift fully into the New Energy means that We as God are embodying God fully into the material world - fully conscious of Our True Self.

*We are no longer trying to **bliss** ourselves out of the world to return Home as spirituality often taught in the 'old energy' ... we are Now embodying Home or Heaven **in** this physical world as well in all other dimensions.*

Index

DEDICATION

This book is dedicated to Ingerid Esme Ferrer Enzo.

Throughout recorded history there have been stories of Enlightened Beings like Buddha, Jesus, Lao Tzu, Krishna and Abraham as well as legendary figured who form part of the so called spiritual planetary Hierarchy such as Sanat Kumara [the ancient of days], Babaji [the timeless master], Archangel Michael [the leader of Archangels] and Archangel Gabriel [the author of The Koran through Mohammed and messenger to Mary about Jesus' birth] ... but today, in the New Energy in which humanity is Now immersed, New Masters of Truth are appearing Like Mooji, Papaji, Gangaji and Eckhart Tolle who are swiftly becoming recognized by millions of spiritual seekers as brother and sister guides into the Light of Truth.

It has been my profound privilege to become acquainted with and now friends with another and still virtually unknown Master, Ingerid Esme Ferrer who is just Now stepping onto the world stage, as the wave of New Energy Transformation swells to its greatest proportions since 1987 when the Harmonic Convergence occurred.

Ingerid's message is simple but profound – YOU ARE GOD. While this does not 'sound' new it is virtually unknown at the level of the Heart-feelings

since at most, humanity believes there is a spark of God in them or that God over-shadows everyone. Recognizing that each of us is an individual expression or facet in the diamond of God is rare – Ingerid embodies this Knowing with every breath.

Ingerid is a living example of Who We All Are – GOD and will one day experience as a conscious Knowing.

PREFACE

Self-Discovery is about helping to
Free the Master you Are - Now' by 'pointing' to
and being the 'witness' of Who you are NOT

I will point to *who you are not* in the *simplest* and most *light-hearted* and *playful* way I can since laughter and simplicity are God's favorite expressions. That means I will *not* be using technical or complicated terminologies from the 'old energy' or any ancient terms or language.

There is absolutely nothing wrong with that, I actually used to follow that way for decades and if you enjoy it, then definitely follow your Joy, but The New Energy in which humanity is now immersed is based on *simplicity* and this book *is* simple.

I will be *transparent, authentic* and as *intimate* as possible using some of my own personal experiences in the 'old energy' ... *which didn't seem so funny to me at the time* ... and how they took me to the so called *top* of the food-chain of success or what success is still thought of in the 'old energy'.

One thing I do promise is to be **straight from the shoulder**, in your face about Who You Really Are as God. As Mooji says,

"I Love you too much to treat you like a person"

Then I will offer what I have experienced so far in this Beautiful New Energy we are wrapped in like a new born baby and how it brought me to the Awareness of the *Freedom* I AM and everyone *is* ... and has always **been**. It is my hope that you will **feel the Love** between the lines as well.

I will also talk about **How** things **seem** to have gotten so messed up

... and What the **Real You**, the **Self** is doing to help *transform* the limited experience most people are having in their lives and the effortless ease that is available to experience Pure Joy and *Freedom Now* in the **New Energy**.

The separated *identity* or *false self* as I like to call it believes anything of value is **complicated** and **hard work**. This limited *identity* as a result ironically endures incredible suffering trying to find ways to make its life happier and easier.

In this book I invite you to *embrace* the possibility that *Freedom* really is **SIMPLE**

... and available to you *Now* ... I can assure you, if you do you will experience the ***end*** of suffering and discover a ***beautiful*** world you may have believed was impossible to experience in this lifetime.

I will also be very ***repetitive*** about a few ***Key*** aspects of the ***instant shift*** from bondage to *Freedom* that is possible for you Now.

Here are the Key aspects I will talk about and to draw *attention* to them I will usually *italicize* these whenever they come up:

-Attention
-The 'false self' [Identities, Attachments and Expectations = Conditioning]
-Witnessing the 'false self' and Freedom Now
-Staying Open and Saying Yes to Everything
-Feeling, Embracing and Transforming
-Listening, Gratitude and Spontaneous Manifestation

INTRODUCTION

Humanity is experiencing a profound *Transformation of Consciousness* from the 3rd and 4th dimensional belief in **separation** through **time** and **space** and **limitation** – the 'old energy', to the 5th dimensional state of the *Now* Moment – the New Energy where Oneness, Liberation or *Freedom*, Abundance, Joy, Love, Peace and Beauty become an actual living experience.

This experience or state of consciousness has been sought after for thousands of years by dedicated seekers, usually cloistered away in monasteries, ashrams or convent-type environments. Now, in this New Energy everyone, whether they are aware of it or not, are being exposed to higher and ***higher frequencies of Light*** that are literally tearing apart their concept of reality.

There is no longer a choice in this, the New Energy has arrived. What is full must be empty for Truth to enter.

Today, there are many concepts or so called **paths** to Truth, all until now taking many years or lifetimes to complete and are followed by many millions of Truth seekers. Most place *Freedom* out in the future, which for the separated consciousness is desirable since becoming empty is another word for *death*

... not of the body but of the separated *identity* or *false self* and this prospect is terrifying to the *false self*, so for it anything that delays this is encouraged.

For the brave ones who choose *Freedom – Now*, **NO MATTER WHAT** *Self-Discovery* or *Self-Inquiry* is the most direct route and is always a *Now* Moment experience that perfectly harmonizes with the 5th dimensional energies now bathing the planet and humanity. It declares quite simply that *You* and *God* are *One* and the same *Consciousness* ... that **YOU ARE GOD.**

Self-Discovery is often associated with **Satsang**, which together mean,

*'standing in the fire of who you are **not**'*

It is far simpler to Discover Who You Are by revealing who you are **not**, than trying to live up to some definition of Who You Are, which is always a *flawed* fabrication of the mind.

Satsang is a *wake-up* call you gave yourself before you came into this life to help bring you quickly back to the Awareness of Who You Really Are.

I will not be *preaching to the choir* or anyone for that matter, I am not a teacher, I AM YOU *pointing* at *who you are not*.

The *choir* means those that are at least *Awake mentally* and know about the *possibility* of *Freedom* ... they are, in most cases already involved in some practice or spiritual modality and *often have such a vested interest* in it that they *resist* a *shift* into the *simplicity* of *Freedom – Now*.

I speak to those who are *Open* to *Freedom – Now*, and in many cases that means the huge portion of humanity that is just now stepping into *the fire of Truth*. You will know if you are one of these billions of souls who have, until recently placed their shaky trust in the world out there but can no longer go there and on some level you have said,

"There must be a better way!'

"I have come to the place where nothing makes sense without You Where distractions can no longer pull me away from Your gaze Where the world

*around me is nothing more than a fading dream
And the masks I have worn fall away no matter how
hard I try to wear their lies I have come to the place
where my Heart aches to turn away from **You** for a
moment I am Home-sick and nothing can fill my
emptiness but You ... Only the eternal embrace of
the Love You Are reminding me of the Love I AM
can restore me to my Self"*

Chapter One

YOU ARE GOD

The *collective consciousness* of humanity has dwelled in a *state of separation* for countless thousands of years. This is the result of what some refer to as *the Fall of Man*, which in Truth means the fall of the conscious *Awareness* of Oneness, of Who You Really Are.

In this separated conscious state it has *seemed* possible and reasonable to state the Truth, as these two well-known scriptural quotes have done

"Hear, O Israel: The LORD our God, the LORD is ONE"

Deuteronomy 6:4

"There is only One God"

The Vedas

… and yet still maintain and live life as if there is me, my own individual identity and there is everything else, meaning other people, animals, birds, fish, insects, flowers, vegetation, forests, mountains, oceans and rivers, planets, stars, solar systems, galaxies and at least one universe … *and*, there is God.

The belief that there is One God, somewhere *out there*, *outside* the individual self is an obvious contradiction of the belief itself. *One is One* not One plus countless other things. This belief has often been justified by defining One God as a spiritual Being and everything else as physical manifestations containing the spark of God created *by* but *outside* God's Oneness.

And yet, everything *is* spiritual. Even science says in simple terms through quantum mechanics that everything is an invisible wave [spiritual] until *attention* is given to it at which moment the *wave becomes a particle* or a physical manifestation, yet still spiritual since it is *within* and created *out of* the wave … Spirit taking form out *of* as well as *within* It Self.

Wave - Particle

Everything that exists comes out of nothing-ness or no-thing – emptiness, and becomes some-thing through *conscious attention* … from the tiniest particle to the vast universe. However, the spiritual nature of nothing-ness is still at the core of the manifestation, which is always temporary, from a soap bubble to a star system, which eventually return to their original *nothing-ness* or *empty* spiritual state.

This means that **Pure Conscious Awareness**, untainted by beliefs, Who has been given the name God and numberless other versions of this concept by the separated *false self*, created everything **out of It Self** and if out of It Self, **within** It Self since there is no **outside** One, which can have no boundaries if it is One. The unbroken line that forms a circle is just a conceptual image to out-picture Oneness, which is boundless.

From this understanding it must be seen that if every-*thing* is a physically manifested **extension** of Pure Conscious Awareness - God, then that which animates these creations must also be this **Pure Conscious Awareness** or **One God**. This means that the manifestation is made **of**, has **within** it and **is** the One God.

Most spiritual teachings speak of God **in** you but do not refer to God **as** you which is a *huge difference* and is an attempt to confirm that we are **not** the One God. This teaching has allowed almost every traditional spiritual belief system to maintain an iron grip hold over its followers as an *intermediary* between the One God and them enacting any rule, practice, discipline or consequence it chooses to impose on those who fail to comply with their definitions of Truth, including the fantasy of **heaven** and **hell**.

If God is **Love**, which is an aspect of It's Pure **extensions** of It Self, then where could anything less than **Love** exist within It Self such as anger, judgment and cruelty. How could God be so foolish as to **damn** parts of It Self to an existence - *eternal by some definitions*, less than Perfect Peace, Beauty, Abundance and Freedom, which are also aspects of its **Infinite Being**?

Despite the obvious insanity of this, the vast majority of humanity believes and fears this to some degree, so great has the *conditioning* been of the horrendous possibilities it suggests.

From the understanding of **all** being One **as** God it becomes easy to also recognize that the only difference between all creations, other than appearance is the level of *awareness* each of these creations has of It Self as the One God or Pure Conscious Awareness. Each is inherently an equal extension of this One God but lacks, to some extent the *Awareness* of Who It Really Is.

From this clear understanding it becomes possible to say without the blasphemous association that the separated *false self* has about such statements, that every-thing manifested *is* this Pure Conscious Awareness or One God. Therefore, to state that You Are God is the *simple* Truth. To say, **I AM THAT I AM**, given to Moses on Mt. Sinai as the name of God, is a simple way of declaring Who you and me and everything else – *All That Is* – *is* … the *One God*.

*"God dwells in you, **as you,** and you don't have to **do** anything to be God-realized or Self-realized, it is already your true and natural state. Just drop all seeking, **turn your attention inward**, and sacrifice your mind to the One Self radiating in the Heart of your very Being. For this to be your own presently lived experience, Self-Inquiry is the one direct and immediate way."- Ramana Maharshi*

It makes perfect sense that when anyone becomes *Aware* of this Truth that there comes upon that one an *expanded consciousness* as well. Since Pure Conscious Awareness – God created *All That Is* out of and within *It Self*, knowing Who it *Is* must also *remind* that one of the Power and Wisdom they have always possessed and Now possess to do such things.

This Awareness then may be further extended into what may be called the ***Divine Sovereign Independent*** - ***You*** aspect of the One God to create or ***choose,*** as I will explain later, whatever experiences they desire ... in other words God-like abilities.

This is the ***Awareness*** that is dawning upon humanity *Now* in the New Energy ... the first baby steps of the prophesized ***Golden Age***.

*"The reason that you struggle is in order **to maintain a sense of a separate self**, a self which is ultimately nothing more than a defense mechanism against the revelation that no separate self actually exists."*- Adyashanti - *"The Impact of Awakening"*

Chapter Two

HOW DID IT ALL BEGIN?

There is only *Pure Conscious Awareness*, most call *One* or *God* or another name meaning the same thing depending on the belief system.

God manifests *universes, galaxies, worlds* and everything in them in order to *play* with and *know* It Self. These are like solid 3D holographic images that are temporary time and space bound having a beginning and an ending and are ever changing which gives them the appearance or **illusion* of a linear 3-Dimentional experience.

God then *extended* a portion of It Self into these holographic-like 3D density screens to *fully* experience It Self. In order to *fully* experience It Self it must *fall in conscious awareness* of Its God-hood. If It was *aware* that the experience was not ***real*, the experience would be diminished by this knowledge. This is the beginning of the belief in *separation* which further creates the illusion of *limitation*.

This creates the illusion of *boundaries* around boundlessness providing It with the opportunity to experience It Self in a time and space world of constant change where It can *taste contrast*.

The word *extended* is used instead of *projected* because Being One, It can only extend It Self *to* It Self. The concept of projection is used by the separated *false self* that believes everything is outside itself.

When God steps into the hologram It tastes experience through Its servants - the *mind* and the *body* with its *senses* ... also holographic extensions. It also experiences through every other manifested hologram, be it as simple and temporary as a soap bubble or as complex and enduring, yet still time bound as a universe. In this way it can be seen that every manifested *thing* is *alive*.

The only difference between each extended hologram is the degree of conscious Awareness of the God It Is. The human body/mind consciousness *later* *transforms* from ignorance of its God-hood to full remembrance of Who It Really Is.

All possible experiences are *created* from the beginning of this game and provide what may be thought of as an infinite *menu* of *choices*.

*"Since the tapestry of all time has **already** been woven, **everything has already been created**, everything I could ever want to happen in my life already exists in the Infinite, nonphysical plane. If there's something I desire, the idea is not to go out and get it [create it], but to expand my consciousness to **allow** universal energy to bring it into my reality [Awareness] here" - Anita Moorjani*

Through the human body/mind instrument It creates nothing New, instead it **chooses** from this **infinite menu** of experiences that only seem to be unique creations. In Truth that individuated part of It Self - the Self Who eternally remains conscious of Its God-hood, over-shadows the **sleeping-Beauty** consciousness of the separated *false self* or *identity* with **inspirations** of **what to choose**. This is accomplished through what I like to call the **spiritual telephone line** called the **intuition**.

The intuition functions not unlike the current Internet connecting the limitation of the separated *false self identity* with the virtual abundance of the God-Self. These choice-inspirations are gradually **tainted** by the *false self's* deeper and deeper descent into the illusionary hologram as it clothes itself in more and more layers of **identity** or **conditioning**.

IMAGINATION

While the *false self* is unaware of the Real Self, the intuition is given little credit or credibility, in fact during the long reign of the **imbalanced masculine patriarchy**, the intuition was largely assigned to what it considered to be the irrational and unpredictable behaviour of the **feminine nature**.

Instead, what ideas and concepts **appeared** in the mind were considered to be the product of the **imagination** and heralded as one of the mind's greatest assets. Much has been written and taught about this mental faculty further puffing-up the *false self's **image*** of itself.

CONTROL

When the Self ***forgets*** or ***falls in conscious awareness*** of Its God-hood the body/mind vehicles it uses to taste experience take-over ***control*** of It's experience-choices. Since the hologram is an illusion or a dream-like game God is using to play in, this concept of control is also an illusion, despite its highly convincing nature. There is only one ***outcome*** of the game and that is the eventual return of consciousness to full awareness of Its God-hood, in this respect the concept of ***free will*** is also seen to be an illusion. The separated *false self* has a ***dream version*** of free will within its dream world.

The fully conscious Real ***Self***, Who is also known as the ***Heart*** or ***I AM Presence*** and many other names, is always ***in control*** behind the scenes of the game but has temporarily ***stepped aside*** on the 3D level, allowing the *false self* - body/mind/separated *identity* the illusion of running the game. This illusion is a necessary requirement in order for God to fully experience It Self in a temporary semi-state of ignorance.

The game begins ***with, in*** and ***out of*** God and ***ends*** there. The separated *false self* - body/mind/*identity* seems to control the game but ends up in the same place – aware of Who It Really Is.

FREE WILL OR FATE

The 3D experience God is having *as* you is temporary and anything that has a beginning and an ending is a dream or an illusion. The return to full conscious Awareness of Who You Really Are – God is assured and will eventually happen ... in fact it already has happened beyond time and space or 3rd Dimensional experience.

This means as I mentioned above, that the concept of a *free will* is Real only within the dream or illusion. You are dreaming that you have free will and you *do* have it within that dream. There are some who will even tell you that planet Earth and humanity is the only *free will* zone in the Universe, but the entire Universe is also *temporary* and is therefore part of the dream or illusion most people call reality.

Imagine a stream that flows through a forest. The forest represents Reality as it Really *is* and the stream represents the dream or illusion. You are a swimmer, an individuated yet One dreaming God-Self who can do what he or she wishes within the stream/dream. You may for a while struggle and swim upstream against the tide, you may stand in the shallow water and watch the stream/dream flow by and you may open up and go with the *flow* of the stream/dream. All these options and many more are available to you and suggest that you have *free will* to do as you please. But eventually, when you do *choose* to go with the flow of the stream you will find yourself returning to your True Home in full conscious Awareness of Who You Really Are as God.

*"Life is Simple. Everything happens **for** you, not **to** you. Everything happens at exactly the right moment, neither too soon nor too late. You don't have to like it ... it's just easier if you do." - Byron Katie*

This means that certain things are meant to happen and *will* happen no matter what. We have all heard stories about people who smoked 3 packs of cigarettes all their lives and died peacefully in their sleep in their 90's and other people who never smoked a cigarette in their lives, lived in an area where the air was clean and fresh and died of lung cancer in their 30's. These lives followed a specific pattern and nothing could change what was to occur.

When I was about 7 years of age I went to summer camp for the first time. I was given the top bed of a double bunk-bed and the kid who had the bottom bed loved to kick my mattress while I was on it and throw me into the air.

Finally, after asking him to stop several times with no let-up of his bullying I leaned over the side holding in one hand an orange that I was about to eat. At that moment he kicked the mattress again and since there were no guard rails on the bunk beds in those days, I went head first over the side.

The orange left my hand a split second before my descent to the floor and my head landed directly on it squashing the orange while slightly breaking my fall. I woke up in the camp infirmary later with a concussion but under what you may think would have been normal circumstances I should have, at the very least fractured my skull or broken my neck. But no, I was released later that evening and returned to my cabin with a slight headache.

If it had been my time to go this incident could certainly have taken me out of my body for good but as it was there was no sign of the injury until several years later when I began to have neck problems. A *stiff neck* can be a *symbol* for a *stubborn character* and in my case that was certainly true. As it turned out I sustained injuries to me neck twice more in the next 15 years which affected me severely for decades afterward, all pointing to the same message the Self was trying to give me –

'Look at your stubbornness, what is beneath that? It's a block to the Awareness of Who You Really Are.'

I will speak more on how the Self constantly communicates with us later in the chapter entitled "The Language of The Self".

IDENTIFICATION

The concept of time speaks of past, present and future and the separated *false self* is created **out of** the time/space illusion by **identifying** with the **past or history** as well as a **hoped for** or **feared future**. This *identification* clothes itself in **individuality** further validating its belief that it is separate.

> *"I am different from you and everybody/everything else. I am born here, educated there, believe this and that, have credentials that say I am a doctor or lawyer or plumber or derelict or tyrant, etc. I have this experience and that expertise, I am of this or that race and color and I possess these things, I am a father or mother and I have these many children."*

ATTENTION

The faculty of **attention** expands our **experience'**, which becomes our **reality** as we continue to place our *attention* on the same things. This concept of reality gradually becomes **who we believe we Are**, our **Identity**.

And on and on the masks go sculpting what looks like a unique individual, beautiful or disgusting, judgable in every sense on an infinite scale of good and bad.

These **masks** act like **filters**, influencing every experience with a giant pallet of uniquely mixed colors in an endless cycle of judgement, which the *false self* likes to call perspectives or opinions but are really the result of an insidious expanding *conditioning* that has taken over the decision making of even the slightest **choice** from the **infinite menu** of already **created things** and **experiences**. The separated *false self* dwells within a **prison**, initially with the bars far enough out of view that it doesn't realize its every moment is manipulated by the devious influence of this masked-*conditioning*.

LIMITATION

The concept of a separate *identity* is joined at the hip with the belief in *limitation* since it is **time** and **space** bound. The history of time seems to validate *limitation* in every way through the wars fought to gain control of this or that from land to resources to beliefs, whether these wars are global or simply within one's own mind arguing with itself. These inner wars can appear in as simple a way as indecision to full blown schizophrenia.

Space seems to validate limitation through the senses which proclaim we have only one planet to live on with limited resources and expanding populations ... there seems not enough to go around. This has not been a daily conscious thought for most people until recently with the addition of global communication systems like the Internet but every separated *false self* has carried this belief around just beneath the surface of their awareness generating constant fear in the form of stress and anxiety that further taints its every choice.

Limitation is a manipulative tool in the hands of those who seem to hold the reigns of power influencing everything from education to provide you with the tools to **compete** for your share of the limited pie to self-improvement gurus who promote ways and means to be at the top of the heap and insure a quality lifestyle.

ATTACHMENTS

When the separated *false self* feels it is *limited* it interprets this as **lack** in whatever experience where it either **does not have enough** or **does not feel it has enough**. Having enough **food, clothing and shelter** form the **basic survival instincts** of the separated *false self* and whatever provides these things becomes the source of a powerful *attachment.* **This is mine** is the first *feeling* connected to these instincts and since these *attachments* concern what the separated *false self* deems absolutely necessary for the continued existence of the body and mind, the *attachment* is so powerful that it will protect it to the death.

EXPECTATIONS

When you are identified with a separated *false self* who believes it has specific needs and *limited* resources to fulfil those needs and a protective tendency toward what they have acquired to fulfil those needs you come to expect those things to continue appearing in your experience. This is the *false self's* focus on **expected- outcomes**, a fixation on **results**. It's a preoccupation on **I have-to-have** this end result. The expectation however, is laden with doubt that this may **not** be your experience and a host of new **fear based tendencies** are birthed out of this.

Hope becomes what appears to be a positive tendency connected with *expectations*. Nevertheless, hope remains *uncertain* of outcomes and has a subtle element of fear connected to it. Connected to *hope* are *belief, faith* and *trust* and since there is an underlying doubt/fear associated with them they are often used in the control of the separated *false self,* most commonly through religious organizations but also found in the media, politics and elsewhere. It is normal to call your particular spiritual **belief** – a **faith**; *"What is your* *faith?"* But religious or not the concept of having hope, belief, faith or trust in something is associated with *expectations*.

The tendencies to have hope, belief, faith or trust *are* very useful on the way to *Knowing* and I am certainly not saying you should abandon anything. This book is not about trying to *change* anyone, it's about *revealing the simplicity* of becoming Aware of the *Freedom* You Are *Now*. You may choose to continue using the 'old energy' stair-step approach to your *Freedom* or simply *go-for-it Now* in the simple and effortless way the New Energy offers – there is no right or wrong here, it's just another *choice*.

Whatever your choice may be ... when you combine your separated *false self identity* with *limitation, attachments* and *expectations* you *suffer*. And it is that very suffering that eventually leads you to the door of

'I choose Freedom Now – NO MATTER WHAT!'

In my own case I gave my *attention* to being *Rich* and *Recognized*. For most of my life I struggled to be successful, to be recognized, to be accepted and to be appreciated, even celebrated. And yet most everything I tried to get me there never really interested me and so the wealth, power and fame I yearned for eluded me for many years.

Nevertheless, eventually I did find something that fired me up for a while and I quickly became a multi-millionaire, a big fish in a little pond and there I basked in the glow of the glamorous life for well over a decade. And yet at the height of this so called *success* I felt *empty* and *miserable*.

I had never asked *why* I wanted to be Rich and Recognized. As a result I had created an *identity* that believed it could be happy if it possessed enough money and enough friends and admirers. But what I really wanted beneath the surface of this *attention* was to feel **safe and loved**.

These are 'Natural' aspects of the **essence** of how we all **feel** when we are **Aware** of Who We Really Are. And when this awareness returns we have consciously returned **Home** to the Truth – that **We Are God**.

*In summary, your false self **identity** is made up of a multitude of **masks** combined with the feeling of **limitation** you get by living in this time and space bound **separated** belief. And the tendency to toward **attachments** and **expectations** that limitation encourages make up the **conditioning** that you have believed **defines** you.*

CHOOSING FREEDOM

So, after 23 years of spiritual seeking and at the top of my so called worldly *power* in 1999, I said:

"I choose Freedom – NO MATTER WHAT!"

I will explain just what NO MATTER WHAT turned out to be for me later.

Then I chucked it all and jumped off the cliff of **Self-Discovery**, the most **direct route** to *Freedom* I had ever found at that point or since. I had not consciously intended to let all my wealth just evaporate but the Real Self had **an open door** now to orchestrate my life seamlessly toward **Freedom** and in my case that required that I let everything go.

Here's what my life looked like. On January 4th, 1999 I had a yearly income that had just hit $600,000 or about a million dollars in today's money as I write these pages. I lived in a 3,500 square foot house in Toronto and a 5,000 square foot house in the country on 10 acres and my business was worth about $10,000,000 according to a business formula my chartered accountant had given to me. I regularly hung out with millionaires and a few billionaires and attended lavish parties in Beverley Hills, Hawaii, Miami and other exotic places. I had it all and could do whatever I wanted, buy whatever I desired and go wherever I pleased.

And yet despite decades of spiritual seeking and into my 3rd marriage, my life was empty and miserable. So on January 5th, 1999 I walked away from it all.

"As long as you are interested in your present way of living, you will not abandon it. [Self] Discovery cannot come as long as you cling to the familiar.

It is only when you realize fully the immense sorrow of your life and revolt against it, that a way out can be found." - Nisargadatta

You could say that I had **lost my mind** but that took several more years and a 4th marriage, this time to **Kali Ma**, the ego slayer - *false self* killer.

It took another 15 years in that hellish world to strip away every layer of *identity* before I fell fully into the arms of Truth and realized that I had always been **Free** ... something everyone can do in this New Energy **almost instantly**.

This simple but beautiful quote you may be familiar with from the Sufi poet Rumi describes my experience perfectly:

*"I have lived on the lip of **insanity**, wanting to know reasons, knocking on a door. It opens. I've been knocking from the inside."*

Self-Discovery is a ***pathless path*** without practices, modalities, disciplines, self-denial, or time bound concepts. It means becoming consciously aware of ***Who*** You Really Are – *Now* and for most people this means recognizing who they are ***Not***.

Self-Discovery or Self-Inquiry goes straight into conditioning, unprotected, vulnerable, transparent and authentic. It goes beyond all concepts of being Awakened only on a mental level as so many spiritual people are. It means being fully open and naked, hiding nothing and feeling everything that comes up that is ready to be transformed.

When you ***accept*** that you have been living in a dream you have taken a very fast and ***direct*** route to becoming the ***witness*** in the audience of your own movie/dream and from that position of *Freedom* you watch but you do not ***buy-into-it***. It's what Jesus meant when he said:

"Being 'IN' the world, not "OF' it."

He also said:

"You will do what I have done and greater things will you do"

He knew Who He was and came to tell/show humanity that ***We Are exactly the same*** as He Is. Oneness is not God and something else – only God, and ***We Are It*** … that was His message and every Master's message before and since. My message is the same and it is the message of The Golden Age,

YOU ARE GOD

Self-Discovery asks us to look straight into the face of this Truth, *Now* in this New Energy, in the first days of The Golden Age with no fear of being burned at the stake as we give our ***attention*** to and ***declare*** the Truth,

I AM THAT I AM

… knowing that ***It*** will ***expand*** in our Awareness and therefore in our experience – ***Now*** … not in some distant unknown future when we so called ***qualify***.

A Course in Miracles says that

"Nothing real can be threatened. Nothing unreal exists."

This means that anything which can be threatened *is not **real*. In this understanding anything which has a beginning and an ending can be threatened and is not real.

According to the **String Theory**,

the universe is a consciousness hologram

and that reality is a projected illusion within the hologram.

The ancient **Upanishads** speak of

maya, which means "illusion"

where things appear to be present but are not what they seem.

What is **un-Real <u>does</u> emanate from a temporary extension of You to You – God to God and appears on the screen of consciousness. As such there is a **real-ness** to it. This is a Divine Dichotomy and cannot be explained.

The universal tendency in human beings is to seek lasting happiness in the field of names and forms, a transient field.

Because they believe this is all there is, they look for happiness by immersing themselves in experience after experience, therapy after therapy, workshop after workshop — even "spiritual" ones, which all sound so promising but never really address the present.

This is really a form of avoidance, a distraction from what is timelessly unchanging and ever-perfect within ourselves.

*Ignorance of the Truth is **the main cause of misery**.*

- *Mooji*

Chapter Three

THE OLD ENERGY SUCCESS FORMULA

Discovering Who we Really Are is far easier by discovering *Who They Are Not*. I will discuss both aspects beginning with the old energy 'so called' Success Formula to illustrate how it blends with the *false self's* dysfunctional version of living. When I say **Success Formula** I mean the way the world has manifested its experiences as the *false self* or identity in the 'old energy'. It's not only about creating wealth, but any experience.

Nevertheless, most people instantly think of wealth when they think of success. That is the nature of the *false self* since it does not look deeply into Why it wants to be successful beyond the 'old energy' fairy tale of happiness. Joy is a flat-line and encompasses genuine happiness but happiness by itself is a roller coaster of ups and downs swinging wildly in a maze of dramas created by the *conditioning* of the *false self,* always **needy, clinging, conditional** and **laden** with *fear*.

The 'old energy' Success Formula has been globally and openly promoted since 1937 when Napoleon Hill had his highly popular book 'Think and Grow Rich' published. It became the template for hundreds of other **wealth creating** books that still fill the shelves of most books store **self-help** sections.

When I first read the book in 1966 I was riveted to the chair I sat in, terrified that if I moved the spell it had cast over me might suddenly dissolve.

I followed the success formula it described meticulously and **did** achieve some fairly significant material success while in my 20's but not the millions it suggested was possible and that I craved in order to fill the void of feeling like I was **unseen** and **unworthy**. As I said, I didn't realize that particular feeling was beneath my craving I just knew that I had a **fire in my belly** to be wealthy and recognized.

The *false self identity* very quickly buries anything that is too painful to look at or distracts it from its focus. Most people don't ask the hard questions about their life until it's in chaos and even then it may take many hurricanes before they finally turn inward to seek the Truth.

In the old energy the *false self identity* is defined by referring to itself as a **body** and a **mind**.

"I am Elizabeth"

"I am American"

"I am a program designer"

"I am overweight"

"My IQ is 120"

"I am black"

"I am Catholic"

"I am a Democrat"

"I am lonely"

"I am too short"

"I don't have what good men want"

"I am a victim"

"I am not good enough"

… and the beat goes on. It's a very, very long list of **masks** that define who you **believe** you are as a separated, individual *identity*. Each mask comes with *limitations*, *attachments* and *expectations* and we recognize these as *fear* and *suffering* leaving us feeling *isolated*, *alone*, *unworthy* and *insecure*.

For many, these feelings are so well masked that they appear in the reverse. For me, who from early childhood felt insecure, un-noticed, invisible and of no importance whatsoever my masks developed into some form of wealth, which I made sure everyone knew about through *arrogant* behaviour. And, what made it even more incredible - not unusual for the separated *false self*, was that I was totally *unaware* of the *arrogance* I showed the world.

I was also a master at name-dropping … if I didn't have what would get me *attention* I made sure I knew someone who did that I could refer to as someone I knew or had met. It was a vicarious existence filled with *bragging*, *showing off* and *putting anyone down* in order to make myself look better. And yet it was a real shock when I discovered that this was the way I *showed up* for much of my life.

When I was 15 years old I was at the local shopping mall looking for a new dress-shirt. I remember the day very well because it was the 24th of May, what we called Queen Victoria Day in Canada because of our connection to England and we would celebrate it with fire-works all over the country. On that day though I had no idea how shocking the fire-works would look like for me.

My dad had driven me to the plaza that day and I was in a men's clothing store when it happened. I was looking at a rack of shirts and standing between what I thought was the front door of the store and the shirt rack. I turned around and placed my hand on what I thought was the door and in a normal forward body motion shifted my weight toward the outside of the store. But the door didn't budge because it was a huge plate glass window.

The forward movement of my body brought my head into contact with the window and must have hit exactly the right frequency of the glass to shatter it because all of a sudden glass was falling everywhere. Somehow I managed to get one foot on the outside of the partition holding the glass at the bottom, so I was trapped halfway inside and outside the store as shards of glass sliced away at my body.

While this was going on, seemingly in slow motion, the shock of the smashed window made me faint and I fell onto the sidewalk outside and there I lay bleeding at my dad's feet semi-conscious until people started to gather around to see how badly I was hurt before calling for an ambulance.

This kind of extreme example illustrates just how far the dysfunctional *false self* will go to get *attention*. Bleeding often means a deep **call for** *attention* and **love.** I certainly didn't go half way to get *attention* that day. **Drama** is the chief weapon in the hands of the *false self* to be **seen** and *heard* and it will create situations to rival the most dramatic Edgar Allen Poe horror stories ever written.

This may seem **far out** compared to the *false self's* belief in so called accidents, coincidence, luck and chance but these things do not exist in Truth ... everything has a **cause** that emanates either from and tainted by the dysfunctional *conditioning* of the *false self* ... or, from the Real Self Who is always in perfect Balance with Truth.

My mother never acknowledged that I was wealthy, and she was right for a long while. For over a decade I lived far enough beyond my means to give me the **appearance** of wealth. For example I always drove a brand new luxury car every year, something that nobody could miss as a symbol of so called success, but my mother knew better. So when I did finally become wealthy and told her so she didn't believe it or acted like she didn't and told me I was just acting *arrogant* as usual. That was the first time that I had really *heard* anyone tell me that and it put her way down the list of people I paid attention to, or so I thought. In Truth, what my mother said or didn't say had an *enormous influence* on my conditioning.

*"All beings are bitten by the serpent of ignorance. But when **ignorance** combines with **arrogance**, then we are really in a very bad state. You have to come out of arrogance. When arrogance goes, **humility** comes. When humility comes, ignorance also will go. When ignorance and arrogance are no more, **Grace** will be recognized and experienced as the Pure Presence of God" – Mooji*

I found many reasons to dismiss what she told me about myself and this *cemented over* the *conditioning* I had acquired *through* her that tainted most of my life until Self-Discovery opened that very big can of worms.

*I will use this moment to make very clear that difficult family issues that for some seem almost like criminal behaviour on the part of the parents are not mistakes. We have agreements with soul family members before we arrive here to **recreate*** *conditioning to be **transformed**. **Everything** is **orchestrated perfectly** for our **Freedom** and placing blame on **anyone** is an aspect of the **victim consciousness** so prevalent in the **sleeping false self**.*

THE SUCCESS FORMULA

So now let's look at how the 'old energy' Success Formula wraps itself like a snake around the *false self's identity conditioning* to bring about the **appearance** of success, the brass ring that signifies to it that it has **arrived** at what it thought would bring happiness.

The first thing to know is that the 'old energy' Success Formula **does work** but that it comes with a huge price-tag. It leaves you **appearing full** and with all that you have longed for but also with the *feeling* of being **empty** and **afraid**. And this *feeling* makes no sense to the *false self* who can **live in denial** of this for a long time, in many cases until its last breath. I am very **grateful** that in my case I recognized the illusion I was living in much sooner.

Step One – A Burning Desire

The first requirement of the success formula is to have a ***Burning Desire*** upon which to place your *attention*. Remember, what you place your *attention* on ***expands*** into your experience. This cannot be a flimsy goal that catches your *attention* for a moment then evaporates the next, it must be something that never leaves the corners of your mind, is always there entangled in your every moment. You must breath, eat, drink, walk, talk, sleep and think about it constantly. You could say it needs to be an ***obsession***, an idea that constantly intrudes upon your thoughts.

Does that sound *Free*?

Probably not but most of the world's creations … remember, they are really just choices from the infinite menu of already created experiences, began this way.

And the Truth is a Burning Desire ***is*** an obsession that ***does control*** you.

A Burning Desire is tainted by your *identity's limitations, attachments* and *expectations* that have *conditioned* and defined who you believe you are. It is *always* based on *fear*.

It's an attempt to *get rid* of the *fear* rather than to *embrace* the *Joy* of your Real Passion, which stems from your *Life Purpose*.

If you doubt this here's an experiment you can use to test the validity of this.

Ask anyone you know to take a pen and a piece of paper and write as quickly as they can the top 20 things they would do or have if they could have anything right now. Tell them to write as fast as they can without pausing or thinking. When you review the list for most people it will be made up mostly of things they *want to get rid of*. It doesn't have to say it directly, it could be as simple as saying: *'move to a desert island'*, which for most people is about *escaping* or getting rid of the life they are currently experiencing.

Have you noticed how often travel brochures and advertisements use the word *escape*? Other fear based words like abandon, rat race, prison, relax and unwind are also frequently used in the travel industry to highlight the life most people are trying to get away from.

A Burning Desire is like a *Gremlin* that appears soft and cuddly when you first conceive of it but soon becomes a monster that controls you as the obsession that it is gathers momentum. And each new Burning Desire perpetuates the cycle of misery associated with the growing *identity* of fear based *conditioning* … no matter how much denial of this the *false self* is in.

Step Two – A Plan

The second part of the 'old energy' Success Formula is to create a ***plan***. The plan is usually very complex and can run into the future for up to five years or longer. It outlines in detail what you intend to so called create and how you will go about it. It usually contains broad strokes in the long term and detailed guidelines on the short term.

If you go to the bank or an investor for money the first thing they will ask you for is a ***Business Plan*** with these details laid out extensively and clearly. The objective of this exercise is to give your *false self identity* the feeling of ***control***, but beneath it and surrounding it are the issues again of time and space which further validate and isolate the feeling that you are a separated individual, alone and totally dependent on or influenced by every outcome in your life. This further promotes fear and suffering.

Control is an Illusion

Control is one of the biggest illusions the *false self* believes in and it is always seeking to get more of it. It believes that there is **security** and **safety** if it has more control and our world is filled with a multitude of ways and means to try and satisfy that feeling, from alarm systems to insurance for everything to monitoring systems on every street corner and in every building to satellites that can read a license plate from space as well as the entire banking system, political systems and the global war machine ... all are about control. But *'anything that can be threatened is not real'* and is ever changing.

The *attachment* aspect of your *false self* is in **direct competition** with **change**, wanting desperately as it does to keep things the way they are. Everything in the *false self*'s world is in a constant state of change and the *false self* is constantly trying to keep things the way they are, so great is its fear of change, even so called **good or positive** change associated with its own Burning Desires. The *false self* is laden with **contradictions** and **competition** against itself and this keeps it in a **constant state of stress** and is a large part of why it often sabotages its own creation-choices.

Step Three – Visualization

Visualization of your desired outcome-*expectation*s is perhaps one of the most heavily promoted techniques offered in the world of *self-help* today. But let me be very clear here, *attention* on Truth is not the same thing as *focusing* on a Burning Desire - Outcome. I will speak about *attention* on Truth more later but this form of mental imaging is not the same thing.

The mind in and of itself is a thought, an idea the same as the body or any manifested thing. Although you cannot see the mind, it's a *thing*, a temporary thing, another hologram that has a function given to it by the Self/You when you descended your consciousness into matter to fully experience your Self. It's *a tool* just as is the body, *an instrument* for experiencing life in a dream world. It's part of the actor that you have projected onto a holographic screen within the God You Are to play out the script You as God have written for Your Self.

When the *false self* visualizes an outcome it is *an illusion imagining another illusion* – a potential dream within a dream. It is literally clothing its dream with another dream taking it further into forgetfulness of Who It Really Is. And when and if it so called succeeds in manifesting its Burning

Desire – Outcome, this serves to increase and validate its belief that it – the *false self*, is real.

"Look what I did, don't tell me it's not real. Look I can touch it, I can smell it, I can see it – it's real! Don't tell me I'm not real!"

Mental visualization of a Burning Desire – Outcome is always cloaked in *fear* and *control* in the attempt to *get-rid-of* something *that is causing the fear.* No matter how altruistic the desired outcome may be. Until you Know Who You Really Are and live in that Conscious Awareness, outcomes are always painted with *the brush of fear.*

This is why all attempts to *save the world* are like moving the deck chairs around on the Titanic hoping the ship will not sink. The new arrangement may be stunningly beautiful but the ship still sinks. I am not in any way judging these or any other well-meaning efforts *to lift humanity out of suffering.* These activities have significant value *in the moment* and should be seized if the opportunity arises.

What *I am* saying is that change of any kind is always *temporary* when the *cause* behind the condition being changed has not been *transformed* and until you know Who You Really Are the cause is **always** within the *false self's conditioning*. The *false self* cannot *transform* anything since it is the cause **behind** the *conditioning*.

Don't take the world upon your shoulders. You don't have such a responsibility. Your responsibility is to ***find*** *and* ***be*** *your* ***Self***. *Nobody can* ***save*** *this world. Leave all to God. Also it is good to know and have this attitude that nothing in this world belongs to you—not even* ***you***. *Everything is God alone. When you know this, all suffering and sorrows will go. The space that remains is your True Self. ~ Mooji*

Activisim

If however, you are **inspired** by your God Self to become involved in shifting an existing condition that in the moment **lifts the suffering** of humanity in some way and this fills you with **Joy**, which it will if it emanates from your God Self, then **that** is in harmony with your Divine *Life Purpose*, as are all Joyful experiences.

There is another benefit in what some people refer to as **activism** … it **shakes up stuck conditioning** on a **collective consciousness** basis. There are many, many entrenched belief systems that are hundreds if not thousands of years old and which manifest in a variety of ways that result in suffering to life on every level.

The *transparency* emanating from the New Energy allows You to see **imbalance** everywhere as the **patriarchy collapses** and this may **inspire action** that **resonates** with your own *conditioning*. The action **helps to lead you inside** where **real change** occurs while it exposes and breaks up the ancient congested *conditioning*. It **does** **not** however *transform* the *conditioning* that must be done within each individual.

Changing the outside world manifested by the *false self* never influences the **cause** that manifested what needed to be changed. Whether it be climate change issues, genetically modified food, world hunger, banking and business and political corruption, child abuse or just restructuring an ego-based PTA at the local high school, the cause remains unchanged when the **effect** is where the *attention* has been placed.

The energy or burning desire, which is a Life Force fire, must find an outlet and if its manifestation has been changed it **will** find another and another and another outlet – history is filled with these shifting energies.

A dictator is removed by a rebel movement only to manifest another dictatorship more corrupt and abusive than the last. The leader of a child pornography investigation is himself found connected to child abuse. A water supply is created in a remote region of the world where it took women hours each day to transport water on their heads and later the company involved is accused of abduction and slavery. The list goes on and will continue to do so until the underbelly of *conditioning* that defines the false self is **discovered** and *transformed*, not smashed, deleted or beaten to death but *transformed.*

If your cancer goes into total remission through outside means such as chemotherapy and radiation the cause behind that cancer, if you **have not** *transformed* it, must and will find another outlet to **get your attention**. It could be a car accident, a stroke, financial ruin, divorce or a thousand other outlets, that **energy-message** will show up again and again until you listen to it ... and in the New Energy it will likely be sooner rather than later.

But let me also be very clear, visualizing your Burning Desire – Outcome **does** work. As I said earlier, the 'old energy' Success Formula *does work*, *but at a huge price.*

Last Step – Hard Work

Last comes dedicated, determined *Hard Work* in the direction of your Burning Desire – Outcome.

Is there anything that has been more celebrated and more ingrained in the *collective consciousness* than hard work? Even before you came out of the womb you heard the background noise chattering away about how respectable, how virtuous, how moral, how upright, how noble, how wholesome it is to be a hardworking person.

"Hard work is not the path to Well-Being. Feeling good is the path [pathless-path] to Well-Being. You don't create through action, you create [choose] through vibration. And then, your vibration calls action from you" – Abraham

Perhaps like me you heard your dad tell you after a long day at work and *feeling* a little grumpy that he expected respect from everyone for the hard work he did every day to put food on the table and to house and cloth the family,

*"After all, I'm the bread winner in this house ...
and look at your mother too, how she slaves away
cleaning and cooking and ironing and sewing just
so you kids can have a decent life"*

Echoes of Harry Potter's uncle and aunt perhaps exaggerated, but not necessarily, who portrayed brilliantly the way many parents treat their children. This is often followed by,

"I'm saying this or doing this for your own good"

The **hard work ethic** is an enormous weapon in the hands of the *false self* to manipulate anyone it wants through **guilt** and **shame,** the lowest and deepest *feelings* buried in the *false self's* list of *identity* masks and the last to fully emerge to be *transformed.* This *conditioning* has been so ingrained in the collective consciousness of the *false self* that it seems like a self-evident truth.

And the media and self-improvement teachings foster this rigid belief through sayings such as,

"Its 10% inspiration and 90% perspiration"

Arthur Schopenhauer, a German philosopher said,

"All truth passes through three stages. First, it is ridiculed. Second, it is violently opposed. Third, it is accepted as being self-evident."

A powerful statement about Truth but it also defines how *conditioning* manifests. If you look at the advertising industry when a new product or service is launched, there is at first a massive exposure through the media of the product and the consumer at first often looks at this with some degree of skepticism since there are usually so many other similar products on the market. They may even **ridicule** it as another consumer rip-off.

But as the media assault continues the new product may even become a short term *fad* that everyone wants and that can lead to a long term *trend*, which later may become an *essential* product that you *must have* – look at the cell phone as a powerful example.

This is how the *false self* creates a belief system as well. A pioneer thinker comes up with a *new* concept, idea or philosophy that seems radically different from the norm and is *ridiculed*. A small gathering forms around this radical thinker and the ideas become a tangible force that won't go away. At this point the idea may be *violently opposed*. But eventually this idea becomes main-stream and grows like a dry-bush fire fueled by the *attention* millions of people are giving it and it becomes *a self-evident truth*. However, this does not make the concept or idea *Truth* – the Third Reich is a striking example.

Hard work as a time honored belief, respected by virtually everyone is another example that is *not* an aspect of Truth.

The *Truth* is *effortless.* There is a kind of work that does *not feel* like work. When you are in *Joy* and part of that Joy involves what we call *work*, it is effortless ... there is no suffering or complaint or resignation about it.

Nevertheless, the 'old energy' Success Formula heavily promoted hard work as an essential ingredient. I remember the founder of the company in which I became wealthy frequently saying,

"When you do something that works just keep doing it over and over and over and over again"

I don't know how many times he said ***over*** but I was really tired before he was done just thinking about what I had to do to keep making my pile of wealth higher.

I can tell you however for certain that for over 30 years after I learned about this success formula I believed every word of it and followed it to the letter. So when I got tired I looked on that as evidence that I had done ***the right thing*** and that I should be proud of myself … and … so should everyone else – another wonderful ***attention getting*** tool. Results or no results, at least *I* was a hard worker!

I am reminded of another wonderful example from Harry Potter when Ron is reading a tea cup and translates its meaning to Harry by saying,

"You're going to suffer but you're going to feel good about it"

That was me … at least my version at the time of *feeling good*. Suffering, the outcome of separation, isolation and pain has been made into something *good* … this is how insane the *false self's* version of reality is.

The origin of the belief that hard work is a normal and essential part of life is the ***original separation*** from God or ***fall in consciousness***.

When we as God decided to step into the holographic manifestations we had created and do this in such a sway as to seem to *lose* the Awareness of Who We Are as God … *the Real Self never loses this awareness*, instantly there was a sense of *guilt* and *shame* that we had *abandoned* God combined with a *hatred* that God had *abandoned* us.

This ***split feeling*** is typical of the separated mind and shows up everywhere as warfare of some kind within your mind, mostly unrecognized but causing inner conflict and anxiety you often can't put your finger on.

UNWORTHINESS

This intense and often veiled original *guilt* manifests as a deeply hidden sense of *unworthiness*,

> *"I don't deserve to experience*
>
> *Freedom, Peace, Love, Joy, Beauty or Abundance"*

it is saying. These are actually aspects of Who You Really Are that you have separated yourself from.

The *false self* cannot live with this pain and so buries it deep within and out of conscious awareness. It compensates for the *unworthy feeling* in part through *hard work* and the subtle or obvious *suffering* associated with it. It is common to hear someone say,

> *"You've worked really hard, you 'deserve' a break or a holiday or to be happy."*

The first place you hear words like these are from your parents or care-givers who represent your first surrogate Gods, so you go on to associate hard work with *deserving* or *worthiness*.

No one is immune to this *sense of unworthiness* while they cling to a personal *identity*. I was wealthy and could have and do what I wanted but I actually price shopped at the grocery store to saves pennies.

I never felt that I deserved to *have-it-all*, that I must on some level struggle to experience the fruits of my labors. I did this almost unconsciously with everything from travel to clothing to dining out. I even created a theater promotion company in the early 1980's called PASSCARD that offered a discount for theater-goers on tickets and dining out before and after theater … and, it was phenomenally popular in the city of Toronto until I lost interest in it … just as it was about to take off.

Something about the *energy* of discounting or trying to live as cheaply as possible made me feel uncomfortable. I had *touched* into my *conditioning* of *feeling unworthy* without knowing it and felt very *uneasy* about it. This is the way your Real Self offers you *mirrors* to reveal what is blocking the Truth of Who You Really Are. I didn't recognize the mirror then but later I saw the blessing of it … even though it left me $100,000 in debt when the company folded.

POVERTY CONSCIOUSNESS

As I said the deep sense of **unworthiness** remains buried below your conscious awareness until you reach a point where you begin to shift your awareness within, usually, at first unconsciously. When that occurs you may begin to feel **depressed** and this can manifest in many ways not the least of which is this deep feeling of **unworthiness** ... you may even consciously start to use words like unworthy, not good enough, shameful, contemptable, useless and many other **degrading** and **depressing** words to describe the despondent feelings that are arising.

These *feelings* can surface at any time long before Self-Discovery occurs but when they are triggered by the deep longing to be Truly *Free* the *feelings* run far deeper, now exposed by your **'Yes – I AM Open'** to *Freedom.*

Rather than suggesting you are moving backward, **depression** shows you that you are **consciously** becoming **aware** of the *conditioning* that defines your *false self* ... it doesn't *feel* good but it's actually a genuine step toward *Freedom.*

I felt depressed almost my entire life and would often think of suicide as the only escape. What I did not realize for all those years was the Real Self was urging me inward toward Self-Discovery and the *transformation* of the *false self*, back to the Freedom I AM – back Home.

Until you do realize why you are *feeling* this way you mask the sense of **unworthiness** with something more palatable to the *false self* like **Poverty Consciousness**. It's far less agonizing than *feeling* unworthy and you are joined by the vast majority of humanity in this feeling. As I said, no one is immune to it and most of the wealthy people I associated with displayed the same symptoms as me, always looking for great bargains and often **delaying gratification** until that special deal came along. They actually felt cheated if they had to pay retail.

Spirituality is the most obvious about a *poverty consciousness* and has made it into a virtue called *self-denial* where the *false self* defiantly uses bumper sticker slogans like:

"All I need is enough to get by ... I am rich in spirit"

... to justify why they are often living from hand to mouth. Nevertheless, living 'as' the Abundance that You Are manifests in a multitude of ways that illustrates that you are **Consciously Aware** you **are All That Is**. The Self knows exactly what circumstances are **perfect** *to live your* **Life Purpose** and that may include what appears to be **austere circumstances**. The difference is, **poverty consciousness** has been *transformed* and you choose what resonates **perfectly** with your Life Purpose.

In the 'old energy' self-denial did have its value since it directed the *attention* away from potential *identity*-building *attachments* by experiencing or savoring the material world fully.

Entire lifetimes could be used to work through this *attachment-conditioning* in the 'old energy' and the Masters and gurus of that age knew this, so practices such as self-denial were often used to encourage the seeker to live in poverty as a virtue. In the New Energy *transformation* of *false self conditioning* of any kind can come and go in a flash.

In the transition from one 'energy age' to another, worn out and unneeded tendencies and practices from the old are released slowly at first and we still find almost all spiritual practices and all religions placing *Freedom* in the future.

This ***unworthiness-poverty consciousness*** tells itself things like this regarding personal Freedom:

-someday

-I'm working on myself

-I'm struggling with myself

-I'm growing toward the Light

-when I am good enough

-when I have forgiven myself

-when I have forgiven the world

-when I have done enough good deeds

-when my karma is balanced

-when I have studied enough

-when I am less material

-when the kids are gone

-when I have practiced enough

-when I meet the right guru

-in another lifetime

-in another 100 lifetimes

-another workshop

-another practice

-more meditation

-more yoga

-more herbs

-more crystals

-a purer diet

-more healing and cleansing

- more, more, more and more …

However, God is *All That Is* and lacks nothing. *Abundance* is another name for God, a facet in the diamond of limitless expressions of It Self. As God, you *are Abundance*. You do not *acquire* abundance as the 'old energy' Success Formula suggests – you *are* Abundance.

If you can acquire or receive something *you do not have* then it can be taken away as well. That involves time and space and that is the foundation of the *separation belief* of the *false self.*

CHANGE

Truth does not change … this is part of what makes it *seem* so distant and unattainable since the world the *false self* experiences changes constantly. In the fast paced technological age of communication we live in, *change* is the most obvious thing we experience. In a single day we can experience what may have taken months or even years to experience in the 'old energy'.

Today we have a thing called *speed dating* to scan through potential partners by the dozens giving them minutes to reveal themselves, which is not possible since they don't know Who They Really Are to begin with. What they reveal at best is an imaginary picture of who they *believe* they are.

Products like cell phones and automobiles are designed to be constantly replaced and the wide variety of options available to us in products like hair and body care for example offer the opportunity to experience change every morning before we begin our day. Change is a major aspect of the *false self's* experience and is therefore part of its false identity.

But change is also part of your original creation as God allowing you/IT to *savor* infinite varieties of *contrast*. The difference is, when You Know Who You Really Are these experiences occur in absolute *Freedom* without *identities, attachments* or *expectations* of any kind. You experience change from the conscious awareness of the unchanging Truth You Are.

SELF-IMPROVEMENT

A whole industry exists that offers to help *change* who you believe you are and make you more attractive to yourself and the world so that your chances of experiencing the success it offers are better – it's called *Self-Improvement*.

Motivational speakers, coaches, counselors, therapist, videos, CDs and workshops have sprung up by the tens of thousands all over the world in the last several decades with a multitude of ways and means to make-you-over.

It's not just the mind that is addressed it's the body too. Body-building and toning, body enhancements, skin and hair products, better eyes, ears, finger and toe-nail products, fragrances, plastic surgery, drugs, herbs and other potions of every kind only scratch the surface of the body redesign, rejuvenation, revitalization products and services available to add to the mind bending, mind training, mind washing services people spend billions on each year.

I made my own fortune in the natural health industry, a huge part of the self-improvement industry. I remember thinking about 10 years into my 15 year career there, *'what does health really feel like?'* Over the years more and more products were added to the company line to make you feel even better and healthier and I took them all.

Finally, it occurred to me that **healthy** was a *feeling* you had when you felt **nothing at all**, just a balanced consistent well-being where your *attention* was not on your body at all. That was the beginning of my genuine conscious questioning of what is **Real**.

As I explained earlier belief in the separated *false self* comes with the belief in *limitation* and that translates into **imperfections** in the body/mind *identity*.

But the body/mind *identity* is a **fabricated illusion** made up of layer after layer of *conditioning* from what you have placed your *attention* on, experienced over and over again and come to think of as who you are. It is laden with *limitations, attachments*, and *expectations* and it changes constantly with each new experience – It is **not** Who You Are.

The body also is **not** Who You Are. Remember *'according to String Theory' the universe and every* **thing** *in it including our physical body is a conscious hologram'*. It's a hologram used by the God You Are in which to **taste** experience through **contrast**.

Self-improvement attempts to **change one dream** into **another dream**. It even uses words very much like that,

"Become the dream version of yourself"

As I have said before, the 'old energy' Success Formula **does** work and self- improvement techniques are very much aligned with this formula, so they **do improve** the *false self's* ability to use the 'old energy' Success Formula to bring about the experiences or **Burning Desires** it chooses but the result is, even if you do so called **succeed**, you still feel the fear in one or more of its many **disguises** such as; an uncomfortable *nervousness* that your success is *not enough*, fear of *losing* what you have gained, *guilt, shame* and *remorse* over *how* you succeeded, *arrogance and specialness*, and in its most fanatical form... *tyranny*...and many, many more fears.

Every new Burning Desire is tainted by this *gremlin-like* conditioning so that the cycle of misery and suffering keeps growing and growing. I experienced all of these feelings for decades and that's what finally made me jump of the cliff into Self-Discovery. I had reached the breaking point where what I had *achieved* and what I had *accumulated* could no longer hide what I had *become* ... that is, what the *false self* or *identity* portrayed to me and the world.

The simplicity is this; the *false self cannot be improved* because it is an illusion. The illusion can *change appearance* to look better but it is still *not* who you are ... and the Real *Self cannot be improved* because it is already *Perfect.*

*There is however **one significant value** to the Self-Improvement industry and that is to shake loose the embedded collective conscious belief in **unworthiness**. Later, the **artificial worthiness** that* *the false self has added to its conditioning can be dropped as **genuine worthiness** is recognized as you become aware of Who You Really Are.*

I mentioned before that most people don't begin to ask themselves really difficult questions until their life is in chaos and that was definitely true for me. Outwardly, by most people's standards my life looked pretty perfect, I had what most everyone struggles to achieve but inwardly I was in *misery, empty, depressed, lonely* in a crowded life and *aching for answers*, with the main question being,

'Who Am I Really?'

"Find your Self and all else will come with it"

- Nisargadatta

"Seek first the Kingdom of God ... and all these things will be added to you"

- Jesus

*[The Kingdom of Heaven **is** the Self]*

Chapter Four

THE NEW ENERGY

I will begin this chapter on The New Energy with an expanded look at a few key points I have discussed.

ATTENTION

First and perhaps the single most important thing to understand about the manifestation of *all* experience is that, what you give your *attention* to *expands* and becomes your *experience* and with the repetition of that experience, it soon becomes your *identity* – *who you believe you are*.

I cannot over emphasize the importance of

ATTENTION

Casual thoughts in a certain direction do not produce anything but momentary results but consistent *attention* on *anything* brings it into your *experience* and in the faster frequencies of the New

Energy it can often be so fast it seems like a miracle.

For example, while driving your car with a friend you discuss a place you'd like to visit, say the Grand Canyon. Moments later you drive around a corner only to see a billboard advertisement suggesting you take a trip to the Grand Canyon. You turn on the radio and immediately hear lyrics in a song mention the Grand Canyon. Then you stop at a gas station and get out to fill up your tank and someone standing beside you at the next pump has a jacket on with a patch on it from the Grand Canyon. This sort of thing can happen in a matter of minutes.

If you continue to give your *attention* to the Grand Canyon, reference after reference will be given to you until you find yourself – sooner rather than later *somehow* at the Grand Canyon.

If you apply this same thing to a belief system such as, *"I'm not attractive to the opposite sex"*, you may expect to find yourself very soon fixating every moment on a multitude of things that make you believe you are **inadequate** for any relationship, lamenting about how you are too fat, too thin, too tall, too short, your nose is too big or too flat, you have the wrong body type, your hair is the wrong color or the wrong style, you talk too much or not enough or say stupid things when you do talk and triggering a long list of other feelings related to your **unworthiness**.

Believing you are not attractive to the opposite sex soon becomes part of *'who you believe you are'* and the world around you will reflect this belief everywhere, on television shows you casually turn on at just the right moment to tell you how attractive you will be to the opposite sex if you use their product, through friends and relatives who tell you that you are too shy or too introverted, through Internet ads and magazines that offer endless suggestions to so called backward, unattractive, lonely people to find the **right** mate that will make their life complete. The Truth is the people they attract will be perfect **mirrors** to show them exactly what they believe about themselves and the agony of that belief system will grow even more painful until they finally choose to look into Who They Really Are.

Attention is the starting point and unless you are consciously **aware** of where you place your *attention* before you realize it – *'if you realize it'*, you have added more *conditioning* to your *false self identity*.

ONE IDENTITY ONLY

A personal *identity* separates you from Real *Freedom*.

You have only **One Identity** … You Are One **as** not just One **with All That Is** or God and your *Freedom* is Here Now. The only reason you are not experiencing *Freedom* Now, if you are not, is because your *attention* is on **Who You Are not**.

It doesn't matter if you know this to be True, if you do … what matters is **where** you place your *attention* in each Moment. If you place your *attention* on **working on** yourself to **someday** become *Free*, then you are giving your *attention* to the belief that you are **not** *Free Now* – and so that belief stays alive as your experience and continues to push your Awareness of your *Freedom* out into the *future*.

You could be meditating and doing yoga for hours each day, eating a Vegan diet, chanting mantras, burning candles and incense, listening to spiritual music tuned to the frequency of your Heart and attending endless workshops and retreats … if you place your *Freedom* out into the future as something you feel you are **working on** or **struggling to** *achieve*, no matter how dedicated you are, you are giving your *attention* to the belief that you are *not Free Now* and that experience will expand forever until you shift it toward the Truth.

*"To awaken within the dream is our Purpose **Now**. When we are awake within the dream, the ego [false self] created earth drama comes to an end and more benign and wondrous dreams arise. This is the New Earth [New Energy]" - Eckhart Tolle*

YOU ARE FREE NOW

The *declaration* that You Are Free *Now* and your full *attention* on this Truth brings your *awareness* back to this Truth and it becomes your *Now* Moment *experience*.

I have found the *simplest* way to *declare* Who You Are is to say,

I AM THAT I AM

I mentioned before, this was a name for God given to Moses thousands of years ago on Mount Sinai. Or you could just say **I AM** … I prefer the longer version. You may have another way to say it but it must be a *present moment declaration* to expand its Truth into your *Now Moment experience*.

The *false self* loves things to be complicated and in keeping with its belief in **unworthiness** believes that discovering Who You Really Are **must** be difficult and **hard work** if it is ever to be achieved.

The reality is, as *A Course in Miracles* puts it so well,

> *"The ego [false identity] likes to keep you mildly miserable"*

This is so you won't be *so uncomfortable* that you decide to do something about it – Now! The reason is simple and lies at the bottom of the *false self's delay tactics* for putting Real *Freedom* off as long as possible … when the *false self* is discovered to be unreal it means its own death. An illusion cannot of course really *die* but while you believe it is real and *identify* with it, the fear of its death is like walking on fire.

This is why we call placing your *attention* on Real *Freedom*

'standing in the fire of Self Discovery'

also known as **Satsang**.

As Mooji says:

*"This fire will not burn you it will only burn what you are **not**."*

For me, the breaking point came when I was so miserable that I was willing to give up everything to be *Free* … as it turned out that was not the hottest fire I was to endure, not by a long shot. Giving up **things** can be really difficult especially if you have a lot of them but giving up cherished beliefs is very much more difficult … at least it was for me. The breaking point has to be so intolerable that you are willing to say NO MATTER WHAT and … stick to that … otherwise when the heat is turned up you WILL turn back.

NO MATTER WHAT

I spoke a little about my material wealth that evaporated soon after I jumped off the cliff into Self Discovery but also said I would explain what NO MATTER WHAT turned out to be for me.

Soon after I made the *Big Jump* I connected with a spiritually oriented woman who lived over a thousand miles away in the USA ... you guessed it, we met on the Internet. I invited her to move together with me in the country home I owned at the time in Canada and she agreed.

This was at first a very refreshing experience since in the world I had just left I had absolutely no one to really talk with about my great passion to find out Who I AM. I had no idea that when the NO MATTER WHAT commitment is made from the Heart, Source energy or God has a sort of *free hand* to begin revealing every block in the form of your *conditioning* that you have placed in front of Who You Really Are.

Kali Ma

Source provides you with opportunity after opportunity to *look at* your *conditioning* so that you can move toward *transformation* of it - a state of being *empty*. When you become *Truly empty* what is Real floods in and you become Aware of Who You Really Are – God.

However, in those first few **authentic** NO MATTER WHAT days of *Freedom* searching I didn't know about that, I only knew I wanted to be *Free*. As a result the opportunities didn't look like or *feel* like opportunities, they looked like a trip down a long dark tunnel into hell. I had no idea that I had just invited **Kali Ma**, **the ego slayer** to live with me and so I didn't become consciously Aware of the gifts it brought me until much later.

I will explain how that relationship acted as a giant **House of Mirrors** for me in the chapter on 'The Language of The Self'.

THE NEW ENERGY is 'Not' THE NEW AGE

The *New Age* can be summed up as a **precursor** to The New Energy, a sort of **primer** to tenderize the long standing tough and rigid consciousness of the **imbalanced masculine patriarchy** that has **controlled humanity** for thousands of years. It helped to **speed up** consciousness to gradually acclimatize it to a much higher frequency than it had experienced for millenniums.

Radical departure from socially accepted behaviour is one way to describe the beginning of this New Age *harbinger* of The New Energy. Women's rights, beatniks and hippies together with radical art, music and dance to name just a few shook up the status quo.

Global influences that began shifting this *inflexible masculine consciousness* began in the late 1800's as the Age of Aquarius began to interface the fading Age of Pisces. This *air sign* influence brought with it *air influenced discoveries* such as the telegraph, the telephone, the television, the radio and phonograph, and the film industry, the airplane and eventually the Internet and cell phones which all worked in the unseen and dramatically influenced the frequency with which humanity experienced life as consciousness experienced a major *speed-up*.

The powerful balancing influence of *The Divine Feminine* energy also began to show up in part through efforts by radical women. As the 20th century unfolded it made far-reaching changes not just in obtaining the vote but also in the powerfully influential industries of fashion and cosmetics as well as for women in the work-place, in politics including leadership of some countries, to women novelists [no longer afraid to use their real non-male name], not the least of which is J.K Rowlings with her enormous influence on the expansion of consciousness through the fostering of the belief in magic, which brings out the child in everyone.

"Unless you become like little children, you will not become aware of the Kingdom of Heaven [Self Awareness]. –Jesus

Major Speed Up

The consciousness of the 3rd and 4th dimensions of time and space is very slow and *attention* on manifesting our *experience* has taken years to be realized in most cases. But now as the influence of the 5th dimension or *Now* is quickly and powerfully making It Self felt everywhere, there has been a *ramp-up* of the speed with which life experience seems and feels.

Transportation moved from horse and buggy to automobiles, to high speed trains and jet travel and altered our lives in a multitude of ways. What took weeks months and decades to accomplish in the past has been reduced to minutes and hours allowing life to *speed up* exponentially and offer many, many more options in every walk of life.

But what is *most important* and has been occurring with consciousness beneath the radar is a huge *speed-up* from the slow 3rd and 4th dimensional reality to the far higher frequency of the 5th dimension. This seems to contradict the *stillness and peace* that often defines *Now* Moment Consciousness and yet what occurs when you speed up consciousness is the loss of *contrast* that must be present for manifestation or a physical reality to appear in your experience.

The 3rd and 4th dimensions of time and space seem to *separate* one thing from the next providing it with endless *contrasts* to *taste* ... and, endless roller coaster opportunities for drama. In itself, this is exactly what you as God designed for your Self when you created the Universe. It is the *identification* with these things and dramas that stirred up all the *kaka* ... still, it was *not* a mistake.

This doesn't mean that when you live consciously in the 5th dimension of *Now* that you no longer live in a world of *things* ... it means you become *multi-dimensional* and experience the Stillness and Peace of *Now* Moment Awareness but at the same moment experience the 3D world you once believed to be real.

We *'live IN the world but no longer OF the world'*

It means you no longer see your *self* as your *identity*, a *victim* of circumstances. You become Aware that you *are* the Self while still being able to function in the illusion of separation without it's strangle hold. This *is* Real Freedom and as a result ... *you get to play* in the Game You, as God designed and created to Know Your Self without the fear associated with *identities, attachments* and *expectation*-outcomes.

But you cannot simply *say* that you are living in the *Now* Moment, that is intellectual Hollywood spirituality. You must *discover* Who You Really Are – the Self – God, before the *Now* Moment becomes your normal way of experiencing Life.

SYMPTOMS OF THE NEW ENERGY

When you experience *speeds-up* you can *feel* very strange. If you have ever been on a roller coaster, you know exactly what I mean. The heart starts pumping faster and faster, there is a feeling of exhilaration mixed with fear and even terror, you may have laughed and cried at the same time and even screamed as a host of *feelings* flowed through you at once. When the ride was over you may have quickly jumped out of the vehicle when it stopped only to have a powerful urge to have another go at it again right away.

The **speed-up** of consciousness is like that and brings on many changes that can be *felt* in a tangible and even confusing way if you don't know what's going on.

Here is a list of a few symptoms you may have experienced in the last few years as the influence of the 5th dimensional shift expanded throughout the planet:

-you don't seem to care about anything much anymore

-you no longer have the desire or need to make things happen

-you have trouble relating to mental and analytical processes. You relate better to feelings

-you care less and less about what people think of you

-the concept of right and wrong seems to be fading

-relationships no longer provide the security, support and safety that they once did

-you crave simplicity

-you experience increased synchronicities

-you seem to savor life more

-you have a huge desire to be creative

-you begin to pick up the feelings of others easily

-you find yourself laughing for no reason

-things you think of begin happening almost immediately

-your physical body is going through all kinds of changes like:

> *-frequent bouts of dizziness*
>
> *-sleeplessness, or*
>
> *-the need for long periods of sleep*
>
> *-you have hot flashes, no matter your sex or age*
>
> *-you frequently get the jitters*
>
> *-you lose your co-ordination now and then*
>
> *-you have frequent episodes of fatigue and spacy-ness*
>
> *-you get unusual aches and pains that come and go*

... and in the area of the mind you have

>*-vivid dreams*

>*-loss of memory*

>*-panic attacks*

>*-random feelings of peacefulness*

>*-periodic difficulties reading or speaking*

>*-time distortions that make you feel like time is speeding up*

-you have the desire to play, play, play

... and many, many more.

It was many of these symptoms and others that I had increasingly experienced since 1987 that brought me personally to the edge of the cliff ready to jump off in 1999.

These symptoms are examples of being ***re-wired***. Imagine that every cell in your body right down to the DNA is like the wiring in your home. If power surges through the wiring in your home that exceeds its capacity a circuit breaker or a fuse will ***blow*** to prevent a fire from breaking out wherever the surge occurred.

You know that your body is taking care of many thousands of activities such as digestion, metabolization, detoxification, assimilation, elimination of cells and the growth of new ones and that you do not have to *think* about any of these vital activities nor are you usually aware of them other than perhaps a *growl* from your stomach now and then or the urge to go to the bathroom.

The body has its own consciousness and knows its function … and, will take care of itself perfectly if it is allowed to. As these higher and higher frequencies of *Light* or *information* or *Higher Awareness* influence your consciousness the *wiring* of the body must adapt in order to flow with them and not burn out. This is the *simple* reason for the many symptoms you are feeling.

WHAT YOU MAY EXPECT IN THE NEW ENERGY

Remember I said that when you live in the Now Moment while in a body you will be multi-dimensional. This means that you will still experience the 3rd and 4th dimensions of time and space with all its *contrasts* and *dramas* but you will no longer *identify* the experiences in them with Who You Really Are.

You will be a *witness* in the audience of a movie called life, tethered to the actor you are playing in the movie but no longer **controlled** by its *identity, attachments* or *expectation*-outcomes. You will be *Free* and yet able to play in the field of dreams you once called **reality** in a consciously Aware state of *Freedom*.

It is possible that this experience **may** occur the very first time you go through an episode of Self-Discovery and remain with you from then on … this is **spontaneous** *Freedom*. What determines this is your own choice to really BE *Free*.

Phenomena

Most people have had what is called an AHA moment also known as **satori**, **epiphany** or a **revelation**. It's a moment when everything is totally clear. It could be as simple and specific as where you left your lost keys and in a flash you know exactly where they are. Or it could be a **Grand Awakening** where you glimpse Who You Really Are in all your Beauty and Grandeur, Peace and Freedom. You just **know** that you are Love, you are Abundance and you are Joy. The depth and expansiveness of the experience depends on how expanded your Awareness is in that Moment.

It is important to note however that *anything* that comes and goes is *not* Who You Really Are. In the case of this kind of experience it can be a tiny hole in the wall through which you get a *glimpse* of Who You Really Are. I am not in any way pointing to *phenomena* as a way to *Freedom*. If an experience such as this comes *spontaneously* then just say *Yes* to it and be *Open* to its meaning but do not *seek it out*. All phenomena is temporary and an aspect of the illusion that the *false self* lives within.

Over the last few decades we have heard more and more reports of *Near Death Experiences* or NDE's, perhaps none more dramatic and poignant than Anita Moorjani's:

"The amount of Love I felt was overwhelming and from this perspective I knew how powerful I AM and saw the amazing possibilities we as humans are capable of achieving during a physical life"

Most NDE experiences are no different than an AHA moment except that they occur usually when medical science says the body is clinically dead. Somehow, the person returns from the *dead* and reports what they have experienced – often with their life totally changed.

The AHA experience can have the same effect and a moment of True Self-Discovery is one of those bliss-filled moments. You just *know* Who You Really Are and this *flash* of Truth remains with you forever afterward. For some however, the *conditioning* of the *false self* draws them back into a semi-sleep and they continue to believe that genuine *Freedom* is somewhere in the future. For others, like Anita Moorjani the Awareness of Who she Is stayed with her and she has gone on to share it with millions of people around the world humbly standing in the full authority of the Awakened God that she *Is*.

I Was Stubborn

In my case I had reached a breaking point where I could no longer live the life I was experiencing. I had achieved what most people called success and I was immersed in the lifestyle that came with it but not feeling the Joy and Peace and *Freedom* I had expected would be there. Nor did I recognize anyone in that world experiencing anything different than me except in the degree to which they had so called succeeded. It was that *deep frustration* and *constant longing* to be *Free* that after many glimpses of Self-Discovery, finally took me into the *audience* watching the movie of my life as a *witness* from the Awareness of *Freedom*.

It did not happen after the first or second or third or, or, or … time I experienced these glimpses of Who I Really AM … it took 5 more years after the departure from my 10 year Kali Ma marriage to finally say *Yes* to everything. You could say my *false self* was very, very stubborn.

Today, the powerful influence of the much faster 5th dimension has reached the breaking point where my kind of ***stubborn-ness*** results in ***enormous suffering***. When you have had a snap-shot of the Truth and still resist falling into It your life becomes a nightmare of inner conflict.

For those unaware of this influence their lives are filled with high anxiety as they witness the formerly solid structures of society coming apart at the seams. From business to finance to politics to education to the military to entertainment to religion, some systems of which have existed for hundreds of years, the cement of the ***imbalanced masculine patriarchy*** that has ***controlled this planet*** and humanity for thousands of years ***is crumbling***.

And this is as it must be, what has been full must be empty before the ***Light of Truth*** can fill the Hearts and minds and bodies of humanity. As Charles Dickens said in A Tale of Two Cities:

"It was the best of times, it was the worst of times"

The 'old energy' and all its structures and *belief* systems are falling apart while the New Energy Light of Truth, Love, Peace, *Freedom*, Abundance and Beauty is rapidly expanding everywhere.

INTERFACE PERIOD

Humanity is in the interface period between the 'old energy' and The New Energy.

It's literally the first few years of The Golden Age that have been prophesized

and it is a ***challenging*** period where everything from the old must be released to allow for the New to come into your experience.

Depending on one's level of Awareness this can be a relatively smooth period ... you are still in the fire but with an asbestos suit called surrender saying ***Yes*** to everything that *is* ... every experience. But for those who are completely *unaware* of the Shift that is happening, it can be a living hell. Literally billions of people are in the latter category and wherever we can extend *compassion* for these ones we should, not because we are somehow *better* or more *advanced* than they are but because we Are One *with* and *as* them – it's a form of Loving Our Self.

The only *seeming* difference between us is the level of Awareness we have in the Moment, of the Truth that We Are God. And still, for most people even this awareness is an *intellectual belief* in the mind and not an actual *living experience* in the heart/feeling nature. Many deny this, saying they are *Free* but their lives are evidence that this is or is not true. The mirrors in their lives attest to this.

Everyone must reach a point where they are ready to be *transparent* and *authentic* and *vulnerable* so that the Truth can

*'Burn away all that is **not** True and replace it with the Self'.*

This requires the NO MATTER WHAT commitment I have mentioned before. Without it, when the fire gets too hot they WILL turn back to the dream of *separation* and *limitation* even though they may continue to **speak** about being *Free*.

For those ones there is a tendency to cling to the 'old energy' belief that *Freedom* takes long years of practice and discipline and sacrifice before **qualification** for Liberation is attained. They may even defend this belief vehemently and criticize anyone or anything that says **spontaneous** Awakening to True *Freedom* is only very, very rare and not to hope for it without much hard work and dedication.

THIS … is not True!

Your Freedom is at hand *Now* and requires only that you look directly into the face of the *false self* and say – **no more**, I say **Yes** to *Freedom Now* – **I AM That I AM**.

This will bring up everything that is **not** True and you will, I promise you, experience miracles of *Transformation*!

"Until you know who you Are, all your knowledge is only learned ignorance"

- Osho

Chapter Five

THE LANGUAGE OF THE 'SELF'

Until you have returned to the Awareness of Who You Really Are – God, You have only one purpose in being here and that is to make this Discovery

After that you are totally **Open** and the God you Are over-shadows It's servants - the body/mind in a **pure union** that shows you, in every Moment *'where to go', 'what to do', 'what to say' and who to say it to'.* It also shows you exactly what your **Purpose** is and what you need to **Know** in each Moment to flow with it.

This is when you stand in **Divine Sovereign Independence** or in an individuated God Self – One, yet radiating your unique Light through a facet of the diamond that is Pure Conscious Awareness.

The Self is in constant communication with It Self/You as you drift in the dream of separation and limitation and for the most part you have been unaware of this except through *flashes of insight*, *hunches* as well as *signs* and *symbols* that direct you to make choices that are in perfect alignment with remembering Who You Really Are.

Since most people do not hear or understand the voice of The Self, It tries to communicate with you through signs, symbols, dreams and the mirror of experiences to point you within

For a long while you did not give any special meaning to these **phenomenal** messages and chalked them up to **chance** or **luck** or **coincidence** if something magical or miraculous happened when you followed that guidance. But as you approach the **breaking point** of your **endurance** in the *false self's* world of **chaos** and **suffering** you begin to get the *feeling* that maybe something *is* going on that you should consciously pay attention to.

Hunted Like Criminals

In the 'old energy' those who did pay *attention* were outcasts and depending on which century you look at, reviled, condemned, tortured and killed. Fear of the unknown was behind much of this ignorant behaviour but religion and its hierarchy often glimpsed the real origin of what seemed like supernatural abilities and suspected that these people with seemingly **special' abilities** would usurp their authority over their followers. Since women were the most receptive to **listening within**, they experienced more of these so called **special abilities** than men and were hunted down like criminals as witches, gypsies and misfits and burned or drowned of stoned to death.

A few men understood what lay behind the illusion of the world as the *false self* lived it but for the most part hid themselves away from the brutal judgment of inquisitions as alchemists or in secret sects disguised as something less threatening or they would recant their findings and accept the strangle hold of the church such as Galileo did who escaped death but was held under house arrest for the last few years of his life. *By the way, he **did** get an apology from the church several hundred years later*

Nevertheless, throughout the world so called **holy people** such as shamans, witch doctors, soothsayers, elders and sages have existed down through history, usually not in plain sight. They had an affinity with Mother Earth and were in touch with the Self offering what many looked on as supernatural guidance and remedies for the suffering that plagued humanity since it descended from God-Awareness into the separated body/mind experience.

Once again however, this was not an error ... it was your choice as the God You Really Are to descend in ignorance of Who You Really Are into the material world of separation and limitation so that you could experience and play in the **dream/movie** of life fully ... to know the **deepest darkness** in order to know the **Highest Light**. The swing of the pendulum is equal on both sides of **emptiness**.

A HOUSE OF MIRRORS

While the Self can and does communicate directly with you through *the telephone line of the intuition,* the average person did not connect with this natural faculty until recently and still with some degree of skepticism for most.

No matter how well you may or may not be connected through your intuition the Self communicates with your sleeping body/mind *false self* through what I call a ***House of Mirrors***. It reflects back to you ***everything*** that is ***blocking*** the Truth of Who You Really Are and It has always done this but now humanity is beginning to notice as a collective consciousness. Few as yet realize that ***everything*** they are getting mirrored back to their consciousness is about themselves … but,

It's always about you

When you cross the threshold of this Awareness you have passed from merely being an actor in the movie of life to being the ***witness*** of the movie as well.

This is the moment when you are *Free, **not of all*** the **conditioning** that has defined the *false self* but of your *identification **with*** the *conditioning*. ***This is a huge difference***. You stop the ***finger-pointing, judging, victimization and blaming*** attitude of the *false self* and recognize that ***everything*** you are experiencing is a reflection of Who you are ***not*** ... combined with some mirrors of Who You Really Are.

Transformation

As *transformation* of more and more of the *identifications, attachments* and *expectation-*outcome *conditioning* of the *false self* takes place, more and more mirrors show up revealing the Beauty, Abundance, Love, Joy, Peace and Freedom that You Really Are. This is why the Master Self can *'live IN the world but not OF the world'*. They can walk through the chaos and suffering of the world, never losing their Peace and Freedom.

This may seem to make them heartless but in reality it makes them far more ***compassionate*** since their ***clear vision*** allows them to ***witness*** the suffering of the blind - perfectly. They ***do not comfort*** the *false self* or play into its hands with sympathy ... they give it ***no attention*** at all knowing that ***it*** in Truth is not real. Instead they *see* those that are suffering for Who They Really Are - God.

GOD Only Sees GOD

Jesus never saw sickness – He saw God in disguise. He saw the *effects of ignorance* – of *conditioning* and He saw the Truth in the one wearing the disguise of sickness. Had he not done this he would have only been *attempting* to so called *heal* in the traditional time-bound ways. Those who accepted his *Knowing* of the Truth were *spontaneously* restored to Wholeness. It was their *belief* in His *Knowing* that restored them. They shifted their *conditioned* beliefs that had created the illness-disguise to the unconditioned Truth through His Knowing.

Looking toward the New Energy, He said;

"You will do as I have done and greater things will you do."

He knew they were *just the same* as He Was/Is – God, but were unaware of this Truth.

How Mirrors Show Up

I would like to give you a few of the more obvious mirrors about how life has *no choice* but to mirror back to you *who* you believe you are ... in every moment because

> 'Your entire life experience is literally a reflection
>
> of what you **believe** about yourself'

This ties in with what I said early about how important your *attention* is.

Until you are totally Free your *conditioning* is underpinned by *self-judgment*, which is a form of deep *unworthiness* and *self-hatred*. For many people this is far too painful to even consider looking at so it is buried in the deepest vaults of their unconscious. Buried or not, it is a belief about who they are and is therefore being given *unconscious attention* and *attention results in experience.* For those who have totally bought into the dream-reality of the outside world most of their experience is caused by this *unconscious conditioning*. They are literally prisoners to it and this is why they will often express themselves like they are a *victim*.

When you turn on the news and see protesters screaming profanities at this or that politician or manufacturer or financial institution or foreign government you are witnessing *self-hatred*. This doesn't mean that what they are saying about abuse is not happening it means they have chosen this way to express their hatred for themselves that they cannot yet look at within.

They may even choose to *become activists* which I addressed before and join organizations that eventually bring about what appears to be a positive change in whatever the protested situation was. Again, this simply shifts the deck chairs around on the Titanic. The underlying cause of the abuse has not been addressed *within*, only the outward circumstances, and the self-hatred has not been looked at and *transformed*. As a result the underlying cause will find another and another and another *outlet* as will the self-hatred.

Again, if your *Joy* is ignited in these kinds of activities then there is a definite Purpose for you being involved at that Moment.

Powerful Mirrors

Bring this down to the family level and look at the arguments, obsessive compulsive behaviour, control, co-dependency, abuse and violence to name a just a few common relationship experiences and you are once again witnessing *self-hatred* directed outward to avoid looking within.

Family relationships are one of the best and most powerful environments to drive the *false self* inward toward Self-Discovery and the Self uses them at every opportunity to do this. Relationships provide a wonderful and powerfully *clear and ongoing mirror* of the buried *conditioning* that exists within every *false self* and offers numberless opportunities to see this *toxic conditioning* exposed. Sexual attraction often helps to keep the union together for a while and as the couple wraps responsibilities and commitments around their relationship the bond grows tighter and tighter and hidden resentments tied to more *identity, attachment* and *expectation conditioning* begin to show up through the relationship mirror.

When you *do* begin to look inward for answers *conditioning* naturally starts to rise to the surface where it can no longer be ignored and relationships show up that provide a clearer and clearer mirror with which to recognize what is ready to be *transformed.*

When I jumped off the cliff into Self-Discovery January 5th, 1999 I opened ***Pandora's Box***, which according to Greek mythology means to release all the ***evils*** into the world. For this reason the myth has appeared as a dark and forbidding choice but from the standpoint of the Self it is the best choice anyone ***ever*** makes toward their Freedom.

Evil is just another way of describing *conditioning* and the so called devil ***is*** really just the *false self.* In order to control its followers religion has fabricated all kinds of horrifying mental and physical images about the devil and its hellish domain but even the tiniest bit of clarity shows you that these are actually *conditions* everyone who lives in the dream world of the *false self* experiences every day.

As I said earlier when I made the terror-filled and wonderful jump into Self-Discovery it wasn't long before I was living with and married to a woman, who for me represented ***Kali Ma*** the ego [*false self*] slayer.

Toxic Relationships

When toxic relationships break up you so often hear things like, *'I finally got rid of that lying bastard'*, or *'the bitch took me for everything but I'm free now'*, or *'he was a soul-sucker ... I hope he burns in hell'*. But the truth is the toxicity goes **with** you to find a new **host** until you finally look within to find it is you who **chose the perfect partner** to mirror your own *conditioning*.

Why do you think there are so many widely popular movies out these days about vampires and zombies? They are huge glaring mirrors for how much of the youth of the world feel about themselves – **walking-deads.** This is not a criticism at all, just the opposite ... it's a recognition of how the new souls being born onto the planet, mostly during these last three powerfully *transformative* decades since the late 1980's, are choosing to look straight into the mirror at what needs to be *transformed*. It doesn't matter that many of them don't realize what lies beneath the attraction to these kinds of entertainment ... the effect of looking at your mirrors and *feeling* them eventually brings you into your *Freedom*.

Self-Discovery turns everything the *false self* says about the world **upside down** and shakes out the nonsense. What looks dark and ugly and disgusting *is* what is being shaken out of the deepest depths of the false self's *conditioning* **to look at, feel, embrace and have transformed.** The entire world and the growing chaos we witness everyday now *is* Pandora's Box being shaken out. The Greek myth also says that what is left when its empty is **Hope.** The Truth is its far more than merely hope, it's you're *Freedom.*

My Kali Ma experience exposed me to the wretched life I had been living. It mirrored the self-hatred I had masked with wealth and power and arrogance and **ripped the carpet out** from beneath my every **false sense** of *security* and **self-worth.** My Kali Ma showed me I *felt* **totally unworthy.** But doesn't that seem to contradict where I had just spent the previous 15 years in the lap of luxury, wealth and influence?

Many people in positions of power and influence and wealth live lives filled with a poverty consciousness. As I already touched on, in my case my enormous need for *recognition* based on *feelings* of being *invisible* and of *no value* provided the passion to become recognized through wealth.

And yet despite my wealth I would price shop. I would compare the price of a can of beans in a grocery store to another to saves pennies. I would see an expensive suit I wanted and wait until it went on sale before I purchased it. I would be sure to shop where I got air-miles and bargain shop whenever and wherever possible. I would select the *special* on a menu when what I really wanted was something totally different. And most of all, I would deny myself *free time* away from my business.

I remember sitting in my home office in the middle of the summer looking out my window at the beautiful weather and longing to be on a beach somewhere or having lunch at some outdoor café in Paris or cruising around some tropical paradise … but no, I was deathly afraid of what would happen to my business if I took my eyes and my *control* off it for even a day. *I owned nothing – it owned me!*

Burned Out

Finally, after almost 10 years of looking into the mirror of self-hatred I found myself walking down I-95 toward West Palm Beach airport, in the middle of a dark moon-less night with the shirt on my back, *pants and shoes too* and $5.00 in my pocket - defeated, desperate, lonely and ripped apart. In Truth, the *false self's* armor had only been pierced and there was still much to be *transformed.* But a major layer of *conditioning* was now raw and exposed, ready to *be **felt, embraced and transformed***. If I thought I had *felt* the fire of Self-Discovery before I was to learn I had no idea what it ***really*** meant yet.

I paint this portrait of my Self-Discovery to expose what my ***stubborn character*** chose to experience - the *deepest darkness* so that I could one day experience the *Highest Light*. Today, choosing *Freedom* and the direct route to it through Self-Discovery is ***infinitely simpler*** than what I am sharing with you. The frequencies of Light bathing the planet and humanity now are ***so high*** that what once took lifetimes to accomplish can now be done in this one life you are currently living.

UNCONDITIONAL LOVE

Then there is the concept of Unconditional Love the *false self* convinces itself exists in a relationship, the reason for being together, the reason for your very existence. However, as long as there is one single buried ***condition*** filtering the *false self's* idea of what love is, it is not ***Unconditional Love***.

"I will "love" you as long as you give me what I want or you don't threaten what I have."

~ Byron Katie

The love you hear thrown around by the *false self* sounds like the title and words to so many songs you hear,

"I Gotta Have You Baby"

"I Can't Live Without You"

"Life's No Good Now That You Are Gone"

These words and concepts have nothing whatever to do with Unconditional Love they have to do with the *false self's* **neediness** based on the **lack** of Truth it is continually expressing. It *feels* **empty, hollow and lost** and desperately searches for someone and something to hold onto to make it *feel* **safe, secure and Loved**. It has no idea at all that the Truth about it is that it *is* Love It Self. As another song says, *"I've been looking for Love in all the wrong places."*

*'The concept of 'Unconditional Love' you hear thrown around like confetti is not known nor can it be known where conditions **of any kind** exist.'*

Unconditional Love is **not conditioned**. It is Pure, it holds nothing to It Self, It is completely Free and extends Freedom to everyone and everything, It is totally **without judgment** of any kind. It radiates Peace and Beauty with every breath and it is never ending since it lives in the Now moment always. It is Who You Really Are in Truth and while you believe you are **less-than** the God you Are **it is not possible** to experience **Unconditional Love**.

When you use the word **relationship** in any context you are speaking of separation, *"I relate to you"* ... there is a **me** and there is a **you**. No matter how beautiful this relationship may be there is still separation and in separation there are *conditions*.

Unconditional Love is a seamless **union**, boundless, borderless and timeless*. It IS Freedom as Oneness.*

Saying that you Love Unconditionally does not make it so, that emanates from the *false self's conditioning*. You can't **make** yourself Love Unconditionally ... you **Are** Love and True Love **is** Unconditional ... It radiates this without words, without thought and without effort of any kind when you Know Who You Really Are.

There is a well-known sentimental Christmas story by O. Henry of a poor young couple that loved each other very much in the romantic way the *false self* sees Love. Before I tell this story let me first be absolutely clear that romance and passion definitely have a place in our lives and are wonderful expressions of the Self savoring Its creations, but it has been given **top billing** by the *false self* as a validation that someone loves or doesn't love and **this is not True**.

Unconditional Love **has no conditions** – romance or no romance, it just **IS**.

You may have heard this story, which I will summarize for you. It's very cozy and touching but there is an underbelly to it that I wish to highlight.

The young couple adored each other very much and both had a prized possession that the other wanted to make even more enjoyable for their partner. The young wife had the most beautiful long hair that hung well below her shoulders and her husband owned a gold watch handed down to him by his beloved father and grandfather.

Christmas was close and the young husband wanted to buy his wife an exquisite hair set with brush and comb and hair barrette to hold her beautiful long hair in place. And his young wife wanted to buy her husband a gold chain and fob for his watch.

Christmas came and despite their lack of money the husband presented his wife with the beautiful hair set and the young wife gave her husband the gold chain for his watch. The young wife had sold her hair to buy the gold chain and the young husband had sold his gold watch to pay for the beautiful hair set. The irony is *thick* with sentiment as well as the concept of loving sacrifice, but here is the *wrinkle* in this moving story, which by the way I very much loved for many years and is called *"The Gift of the Magi"*.

Unconditional Love *does not* involve personal sacrifice in order to express It Self ... it involves sacrifice *of* the personal *false self* in order for Who You Really Are to be revealed. The difference may appear subtle but it's a huge difference and a distinction that can only be made when one Truly knows Who they Really Are.

THE LANGUAGE OF THE 'SELF'

Experience

Your True Self uses every means at its disposal to gain your attention and communicate to you what is ready to be *transformed* ... that is, what *conditioning* or blocks to the Awareness of Who You Really Are is ready to be *transformed* back into the nothing-ness from which is came.

Every experience ... ***every experience*** no matter how insignificant it may seem is speaking to you about Who you are ***not*** or revealing to you Who You Really Are. This may seem incredible but remember,

*Until You have returned to the Awareness of Who You Really Are – God, you have only **ONE** purpose in being here and that is to make this Discovery.*

Let's say you are driving through town, minding your own business with nothing in particular on your mind and suddenly someone swerves in front of you nearly causes an accident and honks his or her horn repeatedly at you as they race away, what is likely to be most people's first reaction?

-what did I do?

-it's not my fault?

-what an asshole!

-who the hell does he/she think they are?

-he/she could have killed us both!

…and other words to that effect – right?

If you did react this way it's perfectly normal, it's okay to express anger in the moment but its how you choose to look at this afterward that determines whether you are *listening* to the Self speaking to you. Remember, *everything* is about you, so what might this incident mean at a deeper level?

In an experience like this you may even wish to pull over to the side of the road and open up to what you really *feel* … to what comes up.

Perhaps you feel violated, unseen and abused. Now you are *starting* to really *listen*. Let's say in this case that what *triggers* your feelings most is the *feeling* of being *unseen*. *Feeling* invisible is a major cause behind someone *acting out* to get *attention* and this can manifest in many different ways. They may dress in a radical way, they may often speak loudly, they may be an over-achiever at work or they may be a caretaker of aging parents, shut-ins or even work in a hospice.

I am not saying any of these activities are right or wrong, in Truth there *is* no right or wrong. I am pointing at them neutrally as *parts* we play in the movie of life that *may* be speaking about your *conditioning*. In my case feeling *unseen* was a very significant *feeling* that I had buried ***out of conscious sight*** when I was about ten years of age.

One day when I was just about to head out the front door of our house to go to a cub-scout meeting my dad came home slightly drunk. I don't remember what triggered it but a few moments later he knocked me to the floor and kicked me violently in the ribs, fortunately for me in his stocking feet. He screamed something at me and my mother quickly got me to my feet and out the door so I could escape any further violent abuse.

I remember limping down the road for about two houses then slowly coming to a halt bent over in great physical pain but far more so in my heart as I sobbed at a depth of sorrow I had never felt before. Something had ***snapped*** in me, a feeling like I was of ***no importance whatsoever***, invisible you could say, like being stepped on as an unseen insect that just happened to be in the wrong place.

Something slammed shut in me in those moments of deep sorrow and a wall went up that later manifested as a kind of stoic –

*"Nothing can hurt me, nothing can touch me, 'I'
can and will bounce back from everything."*

This would take on many different shades of grey as it tainted my behaviour throughout most of my life. I put up a **mask of strength** and was blank in the face of any kind of challenge or disaster. As an entrepreneur I tried many, many different enterprises before I finally became wealthy and each time a business fell apart I would bounce back like nothing had happened to me at all, more determined than ever with a steely grin on my face … to the average onlooker, I was invulnerable.

This kind of behaviour made me *look* almost like some sort of **hero, brave, invincible and courageous** in the face of disaster and of course – got me a *type* of *attention*. The sympathy and admiration was almost powerful enough to even justify me sabotaging my own efforts to succeed. This is how the *false self* creates dramatic scenarios in its experiences that spiral deeper and deeper into darkness and suffering. And yet suffering eventually works in our favor to eventually *drive* our *attention* inward toward the Self's guidance.

The Body

The body is the most effective communication device the Self has to gain our *attention* and get us to listen to what It's trying to tell us. It is virtually impossible to ignore It's many ways of speaking to us and if we are *listening* it takes very little Awareness to recognize the Self's message. For most people however, it takes repeated messages of greater and greater intensity before we listen ... certainly, that was true in my case.

If you get a paper cut in your finger it *does* mean something beyond anything obvious. Now if I heard this kind of information for the first time I would think, *"Crap! That's far too complicated for me, how am I supposed to know what every little hurt or wound means."*

That is where *listening* comes in. The *intuition*, as I have said, what I like to call the telephone line to the Self will tell you exactly what it means every time. The Self was just using this to get your *attention* ... It will tell you what it means if you *ask* and then *listen*.

You may be inclined to say, *"well that's just karma, I was supposed to have this or that happen."* And, you would be right in the 'old energy' but the 'old energy' is time-bound where karma *can* exist. In the New Energy - the Now moment cannot contain karma because there *is* no past … take a moment to let that sink in if you need to because it has huge implications.

The point is, the Self has used what may in fact be a karmic moment to get your *attention* about a specific message - It adapts instantly to every opportunity to gain your *attention*.

You may have been judging something in the news about what **they** did, which is a kind of ***victim-finger-pointing***.

If you take this down the Self-Discovery road you will see how this or any **tiny** incident can reap major benefits in the *transformation* of the blocks to the Awareness of Who You Really Are.

However, as I said about most people and in my case for certain, far more dramatic physical messages are usually required … and often, to gain their full *attention*. Major life threatening illnesses or accidents are very often the **last straw** for the Self to get your *attention*. This same message about *judgment* that was ready to be *transformed* may have been coming to you for a very long time. In the 'old energy' that one block may have been a lifetime mission for the Self to *transform*. In this lifetime *transformation of every* block from every lifetime can occur returning you to full Awareness of Who You Really Are, totally *Free* of *any* blocks … that's how powerful this New Energy is.

On September 22nd, 1998, on the eve of the fall Equinox, a symbol for the death of the old, I nearly died. At about 3:30 AM on September 21st, I awoke in my country home alone, with a terrible pain in my lower abdomen. I had had food poisoning twice during my travels around the world and it felt much the same so I decided to ride it out as I had done before so in agony, I rolled over and somehow got back to sleep.

Who would do that? Wouldn't most people get up … maybe call a doctor? But no, not me … as I said earlier, I wore the mask of being the invincible guy that could handle anything … or so I had convinced myself.

When I woke up late the next morning the pain was much worse but I continued to hang on for a few hours. But when the pain became intolerable, which was a major metaphor for where the *false self* had to be in my case before it was willing to consider going within, I decided I had better call the hospital.

I called emergency and told them what I was *feeling* and they said it might be my appendix and that they would send an ambulance right away. I gave them my address which was on Norris Road just outside town but they heard me wrong and went to North Road in town. Two more hours went by as I lay on the floor drifting in and out of consciousness but when I finally looked at my wrist-watch I realized something was wrong – *no kidding*. I somehow managed to get up and called the hospital again. This time they got the address right and sent the ambulance out again. I was on the floor writhing in agony near the front door when they arrived and they got me onto a gurney and into the ambulance for the short trip to the little country hospital.

By this time it was 12 hours after I first woke up to the pain. If you have ever had medical experience with an appendix you know it's something that should be dealt with immediately.

I got to the hospital and they contacted Toronto for my medical records which took another 90 minutes.

I was given a strong pain killer so I wasn't in too much distress while I waited.

*That was a perfect time to start questioning what was going on ... but while my condition was getting worse everyone around me was acting like it was **business as usual** ... again this was a **reflection** of how I had tried to **handle chaos** since childhood. So I just went with the oblivious atmosphere I was in and drifted in and out of la-la-land on the pain killers.*

Then a nurse came and said they found something in my records that concerned them and didn't feel they could handle it in their modest facility so off I went into the ambulance again, this time to an Ottawa hospital an hour away where they took x-rays and checked my Toronto doctor files, and the hours continued to pass.

It was about 7:00 PM when a nurse came and told me that I would be operated on *in the morning* at 7 AM as the doctor who would perform the procedure was not available. This was a major hospital in the capital of Canada and there was no one available to perform an emergency appendectomy? Do you see what I had manifested as a result of handling any kind of crisis with my usual stoic mask? The nurse gave me more pain killers and a sleeping pill. By then all hell had broken out in my abdomen as I found out later.

*When I got this 12 hour delay information for an appendectomy I should have known that there was definitely a **very serious message** the Self was trying to give me and that I should be paying attention to it. I had spent a decade looking at symbols and **knew** they were messages to pay attention to but now, as I look back on that major turning point in my life I feel the false self knew it's time in **control** of my life was limited and was using whatever it could to distract me ... so, I gave into its subtle but powerful persuasion and took the sleeping pill rather than taking this Divine opportunity to look deeply at what I was being told.*

This may seem almost supernatural that circumstances such as these are somehow **manifested** around the *false self's conditioning* but this is how you so called **create your reality**. In Truth, as I explained earlier, all creation has already occurred and you are *choosing* from an infinite menu what to experience. These choices, as in this case are very often totally **unconscious** since your *conditioning* has been so deeply buried within your subconscious and layered with so many masks that it's like an airplane on *autopilot* for most of what you experience.

The operation finally took place the next morning 27 ½ hours after I first experience severe abdominal pain and instead of a one day stay in the hospital for what might have been a routine removal of an appendix if I had responded the first time I felt intense pain, I spent 8 days in intensive care pumped full of antibiotics and morphine on the verge of death.

The experienced elderly doctor who performed the operation told me later it was a *mess* inside when he opened me up and that I had a severe case of *peritonitis*. By the serious look on his face I knew I was in trouble.

That's when I finally began to go within and ask what the hell is going on.

I literally had to be at death's door before I *opened up* and asked for answers. I slept for most of my stay in the hospital so whatever answers I may have gotten were blurred by the heavy-duty drugs dripping into my arm.

Finally, I was released and returned to my country home with my wife and dad who had come down to be with me during the crisis. My relationship with my dad for most of my life had been a very *distant* one and I considered him to be a tyrant since I was a child. I didn't recognize it at the time but his *deep concern* and his *being there for me* was a clear mirror for the Love I was beginning to *show for myself*.

My dad represented the tyrant *I* had become, a subtle carbon-copy of him masked in *arrogance* and *radiating control* in every area of my life. Despite my greatest efforts to be just the opposite of him it was that very resistance that drew me into the thing I hated most about him. At the time I knew nothing about *embracing* what you hate as the magic-catalyst for *Grace* to *transform* the *conditioning*-blocks to the Awareness of Who You Really Are.

But my *little shop of horrors* had another scene left to play. The resistance to surrendering fully into the arms of Truth held its iron grip on me and that night, while lying on the couch in the living room so I wouldn't roll around, I had another brush with death. I noticed while drifting off to sleep on a cocktail of drugs the hospital had given me to get me through my recovery period that I was not breathing normally. Unless we are focused on our breath for some reason breathing just **happens**. In this case it didn't **just** happen … I had to consciously breathe. After about 10 minutes of observing this I realized that if I fell asleep in this condition that I would stop breathing and die.

Back to the little country hospital we rushed and into another ambulance to the big hospital in Ottawa. A few hours later as the sun was coming up we were told I had been given **the wrong prescriptions**. They adjusted their mistake with a slightly nervous apology and sent me home again the next morning.

The death of the old was sending me a **clear and present** warning to **pay attention**.

If you are looking for the first time at the kind of signals I am describing you may feel I am **making up** meanings to fit the circumstances. That too is a subtle trick of the *false self* to **distract** you away from the **still and silent voice** of the Self. Everything, as I have said, is the Self speaking to you about the **blocks** to the Awareness of Who You Really Are or, as these blocks are *transformed* a mirror *for* Who You Really Are as in the example I shared about my father's display of concern and the beginning of me loving myself.

You do not begin to really *live* until you are Awake and *Free* and until you are Truly *Free*, every moment of your life is oriented around this purpose, whether you are aware of this or not. Many people, especially those involved in spirituality believe that to be Awake is to be Free but that is not True. To be Awake is to be *Aware* of the *possibility* of **Freedom** only. It's possible to live in this dream-*freedom* for many years, even a lifetime believing you have somehow *arrived* and even **preach** that you are to other people but unless you are living *IN* the world but not *OF* the world, the odor of *conditioning* still clings to you and everyone can somehow sense it.

"If it smells like rotten fish … it probably is".

Over the next 90 days to the end of 1998 I waffled in and out of the extreme discomfort I was *feeling* around the death of my old life. I was a multi-millionaire, I had all the trappings of life that most people struggled for and a yearly income that was huge and on the verge of getting much, much bigger as the company I worked for was in a major expansion and I was in the top echelon of global distributors. That is what the *false self* kept reminding me of as the urge to jump off the cliff into True *Freedom* pulled at my heart.

Sometime that Fall I attended a Gala Event in Orlando Florida at a luxury hotel. It was a regular event I had attended frequently over most of the 15 years since I joined the company, held at some opulent tropical resort around the world and I usually enjoyed it very much.

This time however, I was there only in body while the rest of me was drifting in and out of **what ifs**. What would my future look like if I walked away from it all, I asked? I would get half of my sizable wealth and income, I had 3 books already published and I had a few minor speaking events lined up at the Whole Life Expos where most of the top names in the spiritual world spoke at the time. With the foundation of financial security I had and decades of spiritual seeking I had done, I figured I would eventually have a best-selling book and be on the speaking circuit around the world in spirituality. I would be living the life of Truth as I saw it then and I believed that would bring me the Joy that had been missing in my life.

And yet, something was bugging me that I couldn't put my finger on that held me back from making the jump right there and then at the Gala weekend.

The Self knows *exactly* what is perfect for you in the moment and if you are Truly **open**, orchestrates events for your highest Purpose down to the smallest detail. Actually, that happens anyway but the pain of resisting can be enormous. Part of my *false self* had died on the operating table in September, I knew that and I felt it and that was the **final straw** that pushed me over the edge toward Real *Freedom* but the shock waves of that event were still slowly rippling into my Heart and I was not quite ready yet.

*"The instant you genuinely say Yes to Truth inside your Heart a subtle vibration is felt. Don't overlook it. As you become **open**, it will guide you in subtle ways. Day by day, you become increasingly aware of its Presence" – Mooji*

On Christmas Eve something snapped in me. Christmas had always been my favorite time of year and I had a deep connection with Jesus, not in the religious sense in any way but in the sense of a man who had seen the Truth and said NO MATTER

WHAT to It. That day before Christmas was like a *birth* day for me and I told my wife what I intended doing. Then on January 5th 1999, when I was supposed to be attending a leader's luxury holiday in Maui, Hawaii, I packed up my stuff and drove to my country Home from Toronto for the last time.

I had no idea the shit-storm that would follow.

That thing that had been bugging me came and bit me in the ass a few months later. When I joined this company in 1983 I was $100,000 in debt from a previous enterprise I had started that went belly up, so we signed our distributor application with the company in my wife's maiden name. The bulk of our income came to us through that name and the distributorship and its huge net worth was legally *in* her name – oops!

The Self had organized my jump off the cliff through my *body* and a powerful, life-changing *experience* to first of all land me on the rocks below the cliff before entering the sea of Self-Discovery. Mangled and totally disoriented two and a half years later I received a tiny financial settlement, less than my legal bills added up to, and none of my distributorship income or its ownership value. I was like Wylie Coyote after one of his famous attempts to catch the road runner had gone wrong.

The humbling experience was large enough to disassemble but not yet totally eliminate my gigantic **arrogance**, one of my *false self's* most prevalent masks and a huge block to discovering my True Self. It was a colossal gift of Love from the Self but as you might guess, at the time a devastating experience that deepened a simmering depression that had been increasing for over a year and placed a search light on me feeling **completely unworthy** of even living or of having any purpose whatsoever of being here. You may be able to relate to those feelings in these powerful *transformative* times.

Symbols

There are symbols everywhere, we are surrounded by them and if we pay attention they will speak to us what the Self is trying to say in many ways. For me it began with a fascination with numbers.

In grade 10 high school I was sitting in the first day of a mathematics class with a new teacher who taught what was called in those days *New Math*. He posed a mathematical question to the class and then asked for volunteers to offer their answer. I put up my hand and said #3, several others followed with other numbers but none said #3. The math teacher looked over at me like I had three heads and many students began laughing. Then he asked; *"What's your name?"* and I answered John feeling a little intimidated. *"Are you absolutely SURE your answer is #3?"* he added, and I timidly replied, *"Y, y, y yes."*, but then quickly repeated my answer with a little more authority, *"YES!"*... because in this case, I **was** sure.

He frowned at first as if he was checking for more heads then a huge smile came across his face and he looked at the class and said; *"Now there is a student who knows how to stick to his convictions and he is the only one in this class that got the question right."* There was dead silence in the class except for the pounding in my chest as I felt a swell of elation and pride, or what was really the feeling of **self-worth**.

Needless to say I really came to like that teacher, his class and from then on mathematics. He **was** genuinely different from most teachers I had ever encountered in that he made me **feel** that perhaps I wasn't the **rebellious screw-up** my parents had always said I was. My self-esteem was beginning to grow - a good thing in the eyes of the *false self*, nevertheless a very important stepping stone toward recognizing Who I Really AM.

Self-esteem is valuing the *false self* and it is an integral part of the self-improvement industry, which is a huge aspect of the fading 'old energy' patriarchal system. The *false self* is an illusion made up as I will continue to repeat, of acquired *identities, attachments* and *expectation*-outcomes - *conditioning*. Again, an illusion **cannot be improved** or changed in any way except inside the dream it lives within. The Self, on the other and is Perfect and ***does not need*** to change nor does it ever change.

Self-esteem is not known in Truth – the Awareness of Who You Really Are

Nevertheless, the symbol here, which ***was*** given to me by the Self, although I was not aware of it, was about ***self-worth***. I was not ready to recognize this at the level of the True Self Who is always totally and absolutely ***worthy*** but I was ready to recognize the ***concept*** of it. Again, the self-improvement industry has been a ***huge help*** in drawing humanity away from the separated and limited feeling of being ***worthless*** or ***less-than***. It remains now for that awareness to be 'shifted' to the True Self as the *false self* dissolves through Self-Discovery and *transformation.*

As I said, numbers introduced me to the world of symbols and sometime later to the 'old energy' science of Numerology, which became a great fascination for me. Today, many of you reading this will have noticed the frequency that double and triple numbers seem to show up in your life through digital clocks, license plates, sports shirts, billboards, email time stamps ... literally everywhere. 11 and 22 are perhaps the most familiar but now 33 and 44 and 555 and 144 are also appearing frequently.

I will not go into the so called meanings of these numbers except to say that with a little research Online you will find what *feels* right for you. It's important to understand that your Self speaks to you in It's own unique manner, unlike anyone else and that its always best to listen to It.

Certainly be open to what others are pointing to but never *accept anything* as etched-in-stone Truth unless it comes from your own Self as it speaks to you – *question everything else!*

Now what do these number symbols mean to you? Every time you experience ... that is, you **notice** them, the message is different although it may feel like it has a similar tone to it based on your basic feeling about its meaning. For me, for years I would see 11, 22, 11-11, 11-22 and 22-22 and it has come to be a cozy feeling of *being on track*.

This would happen especially after seeing the same numbers in different places within a matter of minutes.

And over time it also became a warm feeling of not being *alone*. Remember, I said that feeling *invisible* was part of the very foundation of my *conditioning* since childhood and the sense that I was *not alone* was like a warm arm around my shoulder from an unseen source. Sometimes when I needed a little boost, whether I knew it or not, I would silently hear,

"Do you believe this is a coincidence?"

I knew that coincidences, luck and chance were just fabrications of the *false self* and that everything is orchestrated perfectly by the God You Are, but somewhere tiny remnants of this belief must have remained or I would not have received these words. Henry Wadsworth Longfellow said,

"Though the mills of God grind slowly, yet they grind exceeding small; Though with patience He stands waiting, with exactness grinds He all."

This means that whatever remains of the *false self's conditioning,* everything is eventually ground down … *transformed,* back into the nothing-ness from which it came. You need do nothing, just stay ***Open*** and say ***Yes*** to everything.

Spiritual seeking can be a very lonely life and it is not uncommon to feel completely isolated. The Self recognizes this and sends many, many symbols to remind you that you are literally and always surrounded by Love, what I choose to call Light … in fact you ***are*** Light, both as the fundamental Pure Conscious Awareness or God that You Are and in the wave/particles that manifest the temporary world you experience.

Symbols so often therefore are simply telling you that ***you are not alone*** and that ***all is well.***

Because this is such a very important knowing to be constantly aware of I will share, what for me is one of the *most profound experiences of my life*. It became both a line-in-the-sand experience as well as a powerful lasting symbol of the Truth that *you are never alone*.

I was about 13 years old and for some reason I was returning from downtown Toronto on the red-rocket, that's what we used to call the streetcars when I was a teenager. I got on the red-rocket and sat on a sideways seat that allowed me to see the sidewalk as it seemed to be sliding past the moving vehicle. That was more interesting on the long journey from downtown Toronto to the bus terminal loop in the west end where I would catch my bus connection home, than looking at the back of someone's head in the normal front to back seating.

Almost immediately my eyes were pulled slightly to the right toward a man seated in a front to back double seat and staring directly at me. He looked like what I can only call sort of Mongolian if you can imagine a kind of boney, muscular appearance particularly in the face … actually, at the time for me he looked a little scary like Lon Chaney Jr. in 'The Wolf-Man' movies of that era.

I attempted to ignore him but his stare was like a tractor-beam, what you might see in a science fiction space movie. You might get the idea I love movies and you'd be right ... they are packed full of symbols and metaphors directed at Truth, if you watch for them. Just think of the enormous influence *'May the Force be with you'* from Star Wars has had on countless millions of people for decades.

Then he did something that today would get him arrested, he patted the empty seat next to him in a gesture that was asking me to sit beside him. Well, even then kids were taught not to speak with strangers let alone go sit beside one, but for some inexplicable reason I did not hesitate for a second, got up and went over to sit in the empty seat.

He said nothing to me at all but smiled broadly as if deeply satisfied and I felt no fear whatsoever, actually I felt quite comfortable, what I would call today – peace-filled. Then, as the red-rocket chugged along stopping frequently to let passengers off and on at every cross street he gently placed his left hand on my right knee. There was nothing offensive or intrusive about the move nor did I even *reflex* at this un-asked-for movement. As I said, this fellow looked a little scary and I should have removed his hand, jumped up and shouted for help but no, it felt almost normal like a loving parent might have done.

Finally, we arrived at the Jane and Bloor streetcar/bus terminal loop and everyone got off. As I was expecting my bus in a few minutes I went directly to the bus stop on the other side of a café situated in the middle of the terminal loop. The man, who I now realized was very tall and muscular in appearance, followed me, stood beside me and took my hand, again very gently in his. He still said nothing.

Again, I allowed this as I would a loving parent. Actually, I would never have done that with my parents since I did not feel loved by my parents at all – cared for in a way but not loved, and here is a clue to why this experience was happening. My life felt *love-less* and if love-less then *empty* and if empty *pointless*.

Then my bus arrived and the man released my hand and watched me enter the bus. I sat by a window seat directly beside where I had been standing with him *and that is when it happened*. The scary man with the muscular bony face and body looked up at me and placed his hand on the window beside me. He stared into my eyes with a *Light of Love* that went straight to my Heart and ***made me gasp***. Even as I write these words *I can still see and feel **that look***. I had never before experienced anything remotely like that look or that feeling nor did I again until my life shifted out of the shadow of separation and into Truth and I found myself staring into the most beautiful eyes I had ever seen since that magical encounter.

This time it was my companion at the time Ingerid, a clear mirror who had experienced Self-Realization years before and had stood beside me for over 5 years as what I refer to as Kali Ma times 10 and helped bring me out of the prison of the *false self* and into ***Truth***. That encounter with the scary looking man was a preview of what ***Unconditional Love*** looked and felt like.

Who was he … an Angel, a Master? I really don't know to this day but it is for certain that is was a ***very clear message*** from the Self that I was ***not*** alone and that I was deeply ***Loved*** and it took me through many, many dark years that lay before me before I opened my Heart completely to Truth, to Love – NO MATTER WHAT and discovered Who I AM.

Symbols come in a multitude of ways including profound experiences like these. Your eye might catch a glint of sunshine on an object lying on the ground and you pick up something with you name on it and a smiley face. A feather may drift in front of your face and suddenly you get the feeling of the presence of angels.

You could be deciding which way to turn while lost on your way back to your hotel in a strange city and immediately see a sign with a pointing finger in the direction you are supposed to go. A symbol could appear on someone's belt-buckle that draws your attention or the icon on a hub cap, or a bunch of balloons floating above a nearby forest. They are everywhere and the Self will nudge you or in some cases even seem to push you over to get It's message across to you. And if one doesn't work it will send you hundreds more until to *do* get the message.

Most messages are subtle and the triggers to get your *attention* may at first seem like nothing but if there is a persistent *pull* to look at something again then it's likely the Self is trying to reach you.

For example, I like to walk, not jog or run for exercise although walking *is* an exercise but I do not do it for that reason. I do it because it gives me Joy particularly when it's around any kind of Nature.

One day I was returning from such a walk and an elderly woman walked up toward me and quickly passed me by. She was dressed for exercise and had a very serious look on her face like she was going to stay as young and healthy as she possibly could no matter what. It was not a joyful expression on her face at all. It was a no-nonsense look that said, clear a path or I will run over you.

I got the message right away, not from her but from the Self as a kind of reminder that there is no physical *cause* for anything ... I must have had a tiny *conditioning* remaining that still bought into that lie.

*It's never about what is **out there**, it's always about what is **in here***

No matter how you may focus your *attention* and living habits on taking care of your body if there is an underlying *conditioning* that you need to look at and the body is the last resort for the Self to tell you ... no matter how well you take care of your body

… the message will still come through in a way you can no longer ignore.

The really big symbols like car accidents, life threatening diseases, financial ruin, family break ups, etc., don't come into your life unless you have missed or ignored many, many other symbol-experience messages.

There *are* exceptions. A child may be born disabled and many people wonder *why?* As you travel through incarnations back toward Self-Discovery and *Freedom* you encounter what some call *soul-family relationships.* It is not uncommon for a soul to incarnate with the sole purpose of helping others to *open their Heart* and this kind of relationship provides just that opportunity. Rather than the *why-me-victim* feeling you might expect, what often occurs is a *redirection* of *attention* toward the *Love* you *feel* when you experience Who You Really Are in some cases through what appears to be tragic circumstances, when the *Oneness* of the God You Are sweeps through your Being like a hurricane of indescribable *Grace.*

Animal Totems

For those of you who have beloved pets, whether you know what animal totems are or not, to occasionally witness strange and even incredible behaviour by your pets is not unusual and it is likely that at some point you may have seen a connection between the way your pet was acting and the way you were *feeling* or in some way paralleled the experiences that were going on in your life at the time.

The Self uses animals, including birds, fish and insects all the time to gain your *attention* about something It wants you to become aware of. Every animal, bird, fish and insect has a meaning connected to it and once again I will not go into those meanings since each person's message is unique and will show up different for them according to that ***message-moment***. You will find plenty of descriptions for each animal totem Online but I encourage you to *be open* to the specific and changing meanings each one has in each moment ... you will be told if you *ask* and *listen*.

I don't *look* for these messages, they just appear and its best always to just stay *open*, the Self will speak to you in its own way when you are ready for a specific message about a block to the Awareness of your True Self … or as I said, a revealing of your True Self that has been opened as more and more blocks are *transformed.*

Just before I joined Ingerid in Norway for the most intense 7 years of Self-Discovery I had experienced to that point, she watched from the front window of her mountainside vantage point as two giant eagles played in the wind over the Fiord below for several hours. She knew then beyond any doubt that we were meant to come together.

Another time I was driving home in the winter snow just outside our little mountain village when a herd of deer suddenly appeared to my right and charged across the road to a field on the other side. My heart swelled as I instantly recognized a wave of **gentle receptivity** immerging from my feminine nature that had been suppressed most of my life. For me, any animal that comes from right to left is a feminine influence since the right brain is considered feminine. The Self knew this and sent a message according to that understanding. But for you the right side may represent a masculine influence since the right side of the body is considered masculine.

Everything is tailored to your understanding … there is no right or wrong. This is why whatever beliefs you may have will eventually, inevitably lead you Home. The only difference is that Self-Discovery happens in the *Now* moment while most beliefs speak about *Freedom* in the future, often the far distant future.

The meaning of animal totems may not reveal themselves immediately but if this kind of communication appeals to you, you will very quickly begin to *hear/feel* what they are saying almost right away when they appear.

I see spiders everywhere and while they do still sometimes give me the *creeps*, I will never kill one if there is any way to escort them outside safely. For me they suggest *abundance* since they are connected to the *number 8* which is associated with abundance and power. They have eight legs unlike most insects who have six.

The specific reference to *abundance* in that moment will vary according to what is going on in my life and I know that it's a *trigger* for me so I always take a moment to listen within for what it is saying.

Not long ago just before Ingerid and I went our separate ways to leave 16 years of cloistered lives, part of mine with my Kali Ma wife in Florida, and re-enter the world to share the message of The Golden Age that **YOU ARE GOD**, a beautiful Russian Grey cat came into our lives for a few months. Ingerid named him Armani to highlight the *abundance* that earmarks the *transformation* of the *poverty consciousness* that has prevailed throughout humanity during the patriarchy.

Armani immediately developed the habit of sleeping on a table just beneath a beautiful statue of an angel we had so we knew right away to pay close *attention* to him. We had him neutered almost immediately but unlike many cats after this kind of surgery he would disappear for an entire day and evening into the woods that surrounded our mountainside home. We knew this was a message of *independence* to pay *attention* to.

When you discovery Who You Really Are, you no longer have a *personal identity* nor do you carry *attachments* to people or things and have no *expectations* of outcomes. You step into what is called *Divine Sovereign Independence* and Armani was there to verify what was occurring. When you are no longer time-bound the future does not exist for you. Certainly, there will be flashes and visions of what is to come and you may even have flexible plans but because the *Now* moment is so fluid and unfixed like the 3D world of time and space, things can change in an instant. Messages such as Armani's behaviour are specific ***pointings*** to what lies immediately before you. For us, since it was a male cat that was a clear signal for me to move on first.

Dreams

Everyone dreams every night and most dreams are forgotten but a few are remembered and if we are meant to remember them this often occurs just before we wake up, even if it's in the middle of the night.

On one extreme, dreams can be a simple release of pent up energy we have stored during the day. On the other extreme they can be full blown prophesies of something to come, even of some world shaking event like an earthquake or tsunami. Many people know someone who had a dream of the death of a close relative or friend only to discover that that they had just passed away the evening of the dream, even at the very moment they had the dream if they awoke and noticed the time.

There are also many *message dreams* sent by the Self and once again it is common for you to wake up immediately after the dream in order for you to remember it. There are many dream interpretation books available but I encourage you to *ask* within for the True meaning as there is no general meaning that fits all. The dream is actually a *trigger* to get your *attention* and the Self is always available to *speak* with you about what it wants you to know if you *ask* and *listen*.

When you first begin to *ask* and *listen* you may find it a little slow going before the message comes through and makes sense but since you have asked the Self 'will' give you many other messages in a variety of ways to reinforce its message and very soon it will become a *second language* for you. The feeling this communication gives you is wonderful and for those who are *new* to Self-Discovery it becomes a very tangible verification that something indeed is happening for your highest good.

Soon you will come to know that *everything* that you experience is *for your highest good* and is *One* with the *Freedom* that you already Are.

"There is no coming to Consciousness without pain" – C.G. Jung

Chapter Six

AVOIDING THE FIRE

Long before we reach the point-of-no-return and are compelled to choose *Freedom* NO MATTER WHAT, we became masters of *avoiding the fire* of Self-Discovery. A normal *false self* existence involves a cornucopia of clever avoidance techniques to evade and delay the day of reckoning when all *conditioning* must be faced, *felt, embraced* **and** *transformed*.

The *'false self'* does this naturally and applauds itself for its cunning ability to circumvent pain at every opportunity.

"Why would I choose pain?" It proclaims, *"Only a fool or a masochist would choose pain."*

However, it's not about **choosing** pain, the choice was made long before the pain showed up in the body or your experiences. The *conditioning* of your *identities, attachments* and *expectations* chose the pain for you, seemingly without your consent but in fact with your True Self's complete stamp of approval since that is the most effective way to become aware of the messages It wants to send you.

You will hear many spiritually oriented people say,

"You don't have to learn through pain, you can grow through Joy."

Pain is not the only way to **receive** the Self's messages as I have explained in the chapter on The Language of The Self. The Self offers us many, many opportunities to receive It's messages in gentle and interesting ways. Most people do **get** some of these messages but the ones that seem to appeal to the *false self* before it makes the choice to **be** Truly *Free* are usually molded by it to make its dream-world more comfortable and appealing, I like Mooji's phrase **Hollywood spirituality** or attempting to **dance at two weddings** – the dream-world and Reality.

After you have made the choice to be Truly Free, **the languages of the Self** will direct you quickly and often pleasantly to what you need to look at and **feel** in the moment but you must still **stand in the fire** of Self-Discovery and that does tend to bring **pain** with it.

Looking and genuinely *feeling* what has been buried within the depths of your unconsciousness, hiding or blocking your Awareness of Who You Really Are, is at the very least **difficult** ... easy but difficult.

The ability to look at and feel this hidden *conditioning* however becomes easier and easier once you *feel* the gentle touch of **Grace** as it *transforms* these blocks back into the nothing-ness from which they came.

SUFFERING AND PAIN

The concept of **suffering** as it relates to any kind of pain is the real bone of contention as spirituality sees it. As long as you live in a physical body you **will** experience pain. The body is needed in order for the God You Are to **taste contrast** and those experiences bring with them a wide range of feelings from pain to ecstasy on every level.

What creates the suffering is *identification* with being a **victim** at the mercy of circumstances 'out there' which cannot be **fixed**, **changed** or **controlled**.

However, when you give your *attention* to the God You Are you recognize that *you are not* your *circumstances* which dance on the stage of *identification, attachment* and *expectation – conditioning.* You step off the stage as a *witness* in the audience watching the play of life, still tethered to what *conditioning* you have not had *transformed* but *Free* of the *suffering* that comes with being a *victim.*

It really is that simple!

In order to discover Who You Really Are by discovering Who You Are *not* you need to be *Free* of the agonizing distraction that *suffering* brings. Being a *victim* constantly draws your *attention out there* toward others and circumstances as the cause of your misery, which prevents you from *feeling* your *conditioning* so that it can be *transformed.*

First, give your *attention* to Who You Are – God … I AM THAT I AM and as this Awareness expands, sitting in the audience as a *witness* is automatic and easy.

RUNNING

Running from what is uncomfortable is the most common form of delaying your *Freedom*. Virtually everyone living in the dream world of the *false self* does it several times every day in ways that become so routine they hardly notice them at all.

For example, let's say you are continuously late for your job or you can't keep friends or you very quickly become displeased with customer service. These are a few of the less obvious ways of running.

Perhaps you have chosen a job or even a career for reasons that have little or nothing to do with what gives you Joy. Hidden within this choice are many mirrors that will expose your *conditioning* but you may be unable to look at them because you are afraid of the consequences of choosing to follow your *real* passion or Purpose.

A typical example we have seen portrayed in movies many times is the artist who followed his parents wish to join the parents in their career field such as the law or medicine or the family business and put their Joy on hold or gave it up altogether.

What is the fearful outcome he or she doesn't want to look at?

Disappointing the parents may be the surface fear but in this case being rejected or seen as *less than* may have scratched the *unworthiness/guilt* wound all *false selves* have that began with the original separation from your God Awareness.

In this case, as in so many incidences of running to avoid the fire of Self-Discovery you are kept in an endless loop of *frustration and resentment* toward what appears to be the *cause* of your suffering. Always the cause lies within your *conditioned identity, attachments* and *expectation-outcomes* but until genuine Self-Discovery has begun you continue to look *out there* for answers.

> *"Living in resentment is as violent as planting a bomb. The difference is just that the violence happens within you" - Sadhguru Jaggi Vasudev*

Continually running from *friend relationships* may have to do with the avoidance of looking at what you hate in yourself. If this kind of running is a frequent thing or if you avoid friendships altogether, your self-hatred covers much *conditioning* you cannot yet look at.

Impatience with customer service may also be **pointing** at your own self-hatred through the conduct of others. These mirrors are right in your face and show up over and over again until you finally say, *"Maybe it has something to do with me"*. This may lead to years of traditional therapies, which may lead to **re-shaping** the *false self* without ever touching the inner longing to be Truly **Free** of the *false self*. As I mentioned earlier, **building self-esteem** simply helps to keep the *false self* and its dream world of separation and limitation alive.

Family relationships are usually the best environments to recognize the messages the Self is trying to send you since you are in close proximity to the mirrors It is using every day. It is also the most common place you run from on a regular basis until you begin to really look at why you are getting the same message-mirrors over and over again.

It's usually much more difficult to run permanently away from a family relationship than it is to leave a job, a friendship or perhaps stop eating at restaurants where the service mirrors your self-hatred.

However, until and if you choose to separate from the family physically you have contrived many ways of running *within* the close quarters of the family unit. You may create your own special space in the house where you *lose* yourself in a hobby of some sort. You may become a clean-freak or engage in endless repairs or home alterations, you may join clubs and associations that take you away from home a lot, you may have boys nights and girls nights that turn into more and more *away* time from the painful mirrors in your home, you may bury yourself in *must see* television programs or spend hours each day in texting or computer games … this is both *running* and *distracting*.

There are many ways to run from the family and its many mirrors without running away permanently. There is nothing wrong with any of these activities … it's the *cause* that *may* lie behind them that Self-Discovery addresses.

In my case, I chose the ultimate running scenario. I departed the marriage whether licensed or common-law … 6 times. That's right SIX! Not much grey area there … talk about fear of facing my *conditioning*. So if it sounds as if it can be really difficult I *do* know where you are coming from. The truth is though, once I got into it I couldn't get enough and despite the discomfort of feeling every gremlin-like *identification, attachment* and *expectation* I had an insatiable appetite for it once I saw how quickly *Grace transformed* these illusionary demons and lifted weight after weight from my Heart.

Few *running* scenarios in a close family relationship, even if confronted and looked at lead much below the surface of the painful mirrors and at best end up in a list of compromises that the *false self* refers to as a ***responsible, well-adjusted family***. The *false self* has a laundry list of packages to bind up wounds in neat controllable bundles to keep its secret life of *separation, limitation* and *illusions* hidden!

> *"The ego [false self] likes to keep you mildly miserable" – a Course in Miracles*

Its only when you can no longer ***take it*** - the dream, that you chose Freedom NO MATTER WHAT.

My childhood was like a third world war, my parents chose to shout, scream throw things around, smash walls and in my case use physical abuse to avoid their mirrors. Souls who have chosen to *transform* all *conditioning* from past lives in ***this*** lifetime choose families where every ***issue*** could be re-created so that each one would lie close to the surface for ***discovery*** later in life when the True

inner work would begin. The family members who **signed on** for this kind of life, usually soul family members, *hold a deep Love for the players* on the stage and play their often **antagonizing** roles with the **deepest compassion** beyond the veil of their awareness.

DISTRACTION/DELAY

Distraction/delay is a favorite of spiritually oriented people when it comes to the concept of being *Free - Now*. If you take a close look at virtually every spiritual practice, procedure, belief system, modality or method of attaining your *Freedom* or Liberation as it was known in the 'old energy' you will find words like, growing, working on yourself, becoming, achieving, releasing, healing, accomplishing, realizing, conquering and even succeeding. All these terms and many more speak of **time and space** in the world of **separation** that the *false self* lives within.

As I have said before, if the *false self* achieves *Freedom* ... it literally ceases to exist. How truly motivated do you feel it is about that prospect? This is why the death of the personal *identity*, the *false self*, not the body, is at the bottom of every fear, whether one is seeking *Freedom* consciously or not. Everything the *false self* thinks, does and acts on has within it a subtle or not so subtle fear of the death of its *identity* and it will avoid this at all costs, at first very subtly but once you get close to your *Freedom* – openly and even viciously.

Here are some of the things the *false self* says to itself that keeps it swimming in its own *conditioning* ... stark reminders that it ***exists***.

-I'm a **loser**

-I'm **invisible**

-Everything **happens** to me

-I can never get a **break**

-I'm always **broke**

-I'm too **fat**

-I'm not **pretty** enough

-I had a **terrible** childhood

-I am **worthless**

-I'm a target for **abuse**

-The big companies **control** everything in my life

-I can't seem to get into a good **relationship**

-I don't **trust** anyone

… and on and on the separated *victim* talk goes.

This kind of self talk is the foundation of the *conditioning* that makes up the false self's **Identity Prison** … despite the misery *attached* to this prison, that goes on to manifest the **experiences** that match these statements – what it calls **reality**.

While the self talk **perpetuates** these *feelings*, the action it takes is directly involved in **removing** these *feelings* and that is why anything that makes it *feel alive*, **important** and of **value** is very attractive. Its part of the **inner conflict** that goes on beneath the surface every moment of its false existence.

The entire **self-improvement** industry is focused on making the *false self feel more alive*, **safe, real and important**. For example, you can see this validated throughout the world if you look at how humanity worships celebrities today, they are the modern world's version of gods.

Again, this is not judgment but how the Self **witnesses** the movie of its tethered experience in the world of separation and limitation **without the suffering** that accompanies *identifying* with these experiences.

In fact this hero worship of celebrities is so **obvious** now that it shows how the collective consciousness is **open** to **exposing** its dysfunctional *conditioning* through crystal clear mirrors that it cannot miss. The widespread popularity of so called **reality** shows illustrates just how non-sensical the *false self's* version of reality is. Beneath the often harsh appearance of world experience is the Self orchestrating events perfectly to bring conscious *attention* toward *transformation* of *conditioning*.

When life is fun and seems to be moving in an upward cycle for the *false self*, it is virtually impossible for the Self to get through the messages it would have you hear. This false Joy is one of the **subtlest** and most **insidious distractions** to becoming Aware of your real *Freedom*.

But it is not the false self that seeks Freedom, it is consciousness.

An even more subtle and far more difficult distraction to become aware of exists in the spiritual community, which I call the **smell the roses** distraction.

When someone has oriented their lives totally to spirituality and the eventual *Freedom* it seems to promise, the contrast between the visible world and the world painted by various spiritual traditions is vast. At first it feels all warm and fuzzy and most devotees devour it's teachings like a starving beggar who has just been presented with a feast of tasty delights.

When I was first introduced to spirituality in 1976 I had a coffee table at Home with over 20 bookmarked volumes that I was reading simultaneously. My appetite for this wonderful **new** world was insatiable.

After a while most sincere devotees settle into a belief or tradition usually combined with some disciplines or practices designed to realign their *attention* toward actual and **eventual** *Freedom* or Liberation from the illusion of the world they have lived until then. Others fall back into their daily routines and **put off** any serious *attention* toward their new found interest giving themselves a host of **distraction/delay** tactics before they have the time to give it serious *attention*.

I mentioned several of these distractions in an earlier chapter such as; *'someday when the kids are gone, when I am less material and when I meet the right guru'.* The Truth is you give *attention* to what interests you the most and as long as the dream world holds enough appeal and the pain and suffering in it has not reached an intolerable level, you will continue to play in the field of illusions … and that is exactly why you as God created this world – to Play.

That is how it has been until now. However the eons of playing, unaware of Who You Really Are have ended and everyone must now turn within and *discover* this. All world events and experience-mirrors are turned on *high* now for this purpose.

Back to the *smell the roses* distraction … there is a kind of dream within the dream *trap* that many devotees fall into and it begins to reveal itself when they speak in a certain way when looking at their *conditioning* gets too close for comfort. Let's say you are having a conversation about some issues involving your childhood and it triggers a painful memory. If you are *not* ready to go below *smelling the roses* of the warm and fuzzy aspect of spirituality, in the middle of the conversation you may distract by saying something like;

-look at the beautiful sunset, it's a gift from God-we are so blessed to know each, isn't it wonderful. or

-let's say a prayer for everyone who is _____, or

-I just love how you've decorated you home with God's Love

These kinds of words **are** oriented around a loving nature so as I said this is very **subtle**. If you are watching this kind of distraction you may recognize it as something that just **smells 'off'**. The conversation may have been headed straight toward some deeply buried *conditioning* and it's just too uncomfortable to go there so a **bumper sticker** spiritual phrase was used by the *false self* to instantly distract *attention* away from the fire.

This is, as I said a dream within a dream, the one distracting believes they are going with the flow by saying and or doing something that sounds and feels **spiritual** but they have not yet made the *Freedom –* NO MATTER WHAT commitment to themselves so their Self-Discovery is only superficial and gets halted when the fire gets too hot.

There is no fault here nor is there with any **distraction/delays**, everyone reaches their level of intolerance for the dream world in their own way.

For me, the frustration with my dream world had to be *very extreme* and many jolts had to be applied such as my near death appendix episode before I was ready to make the big jump.

SEDATING

Sedating is a quick way of *running* and *distracting* without necessarily acting out either of those ways of avoiding the fire of Self-Discovery. Consider people at a party after they have consumed a few drinks. Many people *open up* and allow suppressed *feelings* to be exposed. Tensions, longings, stress, doubts, suspicions, anger, rage and hatred are a few of the most obvious ways people *expose* what they have been holding within ... in some cases so far beneath the surface that they surprise themselves at what they are saying and doing.

In those cases the sedating can have just the opposite effect of what the *false self* was trying to do. It can actually begin to reveal the tip of the iceberg of the *conditioning* that lies much deeper down. And in some of these instances this can lead to a deeper examination of what came up and serve the higher purpose of Self-Discovery ... but in most cases the risk the *false self* took of being exposed was worth it. The behaviour it expresses usually confirms for the *false self* that they are *less-than*, *weak*, and **unworthy** but within a muffled kind of pain that is more acceptable than full-on facing these *conditions* that partially defines the *false self identity*.

Full blown addiction illustrates just how far the *false self* will go to hide its *identity*. The prevalence of sedation-type addictions, which also includes a multitude of prescription addictions illustrates just how desperate the collective consciousness of the *false self* has become of being exposed globally.

The powerful consciousness *transformative* energies that are being downloaded onto the planet to an increasing extent for about the last three decades and particularly Now as we enter the first few steps of The Golden Age – New Energy are violently **shaking** what has been stuck in the **patriarchal imbalanced masculine** energies we have been living in. As a result what was very well hidden beneath many, many masks of fear has now become **transparent** as a result the pain of the collective *false self* being **exposed** is directly behind the massive increase in the drug trade we have seen for a few decades.

No matter what may be done on the surface to try and control this kind of activity, as long as there is a *demand*, there is *somehow* a supply and the demand is motivated by the *false self's* attempt to smother the pain of the *conditioning* that is now rising to the surface very quickly.

Sedating is also often used by those who need **grounding**. They come **in** *with their heads **fully** in the clouds* and find it very difficult to live in the lower frequencies of the 3D dream world of separation and limitation. Many musicians, poets, authors and a variety of artists often have a history of drug, alcohol and sex abuse to name a few. There are many notable examples in the entertainment field who have spent the greater portion of their adult life addicted to one form of drug or another.

Many of these highly notable artists believe that some forms of sedation such as hallucinogenic drugs **open them up** to their creative genius but being **open** is their natural state. They waffle on the edge of multidimensionality all the time and every form of sedation has the effect of muffling the high stress of **wiring** that does not yet resonate with the high frequencies that are **normal** for them.

The inspiration pouring through them cannot **yet** flow easily through their bodies and experience so they seek some form of sedation to dampen the pain and confused energies and filter the intensity of the higher vibrations they are receiving.

The body must be vibrating at a sufficiently high vibration in order to **handle the load** of a high frequency energy and many have not been able to do this without sedating ... just like the wiring of a house and the circuit breaker analogy I referred to earlier. The sedation temporarily tones down and balances the conflict of **mixing dimensions** but leaves **scars** behind in the body which make it more and more vulnerable to exhaustion and breakdown when the higher vibrations are flowing.

This is why many artistic people seem to wear a mask of pain, often disguised as anger, rage, arrogance, sarcasm, cynicism and abusiveness ... all attempts to hide the depth of fear and frustration they are feeling living in a dimension where they are unable to fully express what they are feeling. These have been the forerunners, the harbingers of a **totally consciously aware** God in a physical body ... the promised Heaven on Earth. Why wouldn't they take the plunge into a little hell for that Grand and Beautiful experience we will all soon share?

Sedating with hallucinogenics is a very effective way to **smooth** conditioning temporarily. It does not *open up* higher dimensions, it *reveals* what you are already and always standing in *as* You. You may say, *"So what, it works!"* ... but what happens is a dependency on the *temporary* which is a core definition of *separation* and does not address the *conditioning* which, through Self-Discovery, *transforms* it back into the nothing-ness from which is came.

Until one in this situation examines their *false self's conditioning* these tendencies continue. For most, at best the therapy they usually choose is *rehab*, which is a way of attempting to *control* their habits. Most such therapies advise their patients to *admit* that they are alcoholics or drug addicts as a way of releasing their denial.

They are no such thing! They are God, sleeping.

Only the discovery of Who You Really Are *transforms* the blocks that keep the body vibrating at a frequency lower than the incoming energies, in this case called *inspiration*.

Attempting to *manage* or *control* imbalanced energy simply *shifts* its effects somewhere else. Alcohol or drugs may be traded for tyranny in the workplace or abusiveness in relationships or symptoms of dictatorship on a small or even large scale. If outer symptoms do not appear, inner mental imbalances may be going on such as paranoia, delusions, obsessive behaviour and a host of others.

When you finally make the choice to be *Free* – NO MATTER WHAT, you become increasingly *transparent* and gradually let go of your resistance to looking at the deeper aspects of your *conditioning* that are blocking your awareness of Who You Really Are. This allows energies to flow that *transform* the cells of your body and DNA so that it can effortlessly resonate with **higher and higher vibrations**.

When you become aware of Who You Really Are – God, you become **consciously multi-dimensional** and can vibrate on **many levels** simultaneously … eventually on **all** so called levels. We see this in the **savant-like** children that are showing up everywhere now whose bodies are already resonating with the higher frequencies as they are born into this New Energy.

No matter what method the *false self* uses to **avoid** the fire of discovering who it is **not**, when you arrive at the moment when you have *had enough*, miracles literally fall in your lap. The *running*, *distracting/delaying* and *sedating* are faced for what they are and sooner or later are dropped. You make the choice to be *Free* NO MATTER WHAT and deep within you say, *Yes, bring it on* … and that opens you up immediately to a flood of *conditioning* to *feel, embrace* and have *transformed*.

It's important and encouraging to remember though that once you have given yourself this incredible *gift* you will very quickly find yourself in the *audience* as a *witness* to your tethered *false self* on the stage of its dream world *Knowing* that it is *not* who you are and from that *Free* **perspective**, the layers of *conditioning* fall away like dried leaves from the trees in Autumn.

Once you consciously know you are free, desires will arise, but they will not have a ground, because these will be roasted seeds. They will not have sprouted in memory. You will already know the end.

Only an instant is required for this recognition. Once only. Just a moment. Look into and recognize yourself within this instant. You don't need a long program spread over years to recognize this Freedom. You are already Free. It is only recognition [Awareness] that isn't there, that you are postponing it. You must recognize your own nature [Self] or you will not be happy.

~ Papaji

Chapter Seven

SELF DISCOVERY

*Self-Discovery is Self-Inquiry, it is a deep inner questioning to find out Who You Really Are by looking at who you are **not***

It is not enough to say that God is within me, Truth flows through me, the spark of God lives in me or a hundred other affirmations or mantras the *false self* utters, this gives *attention* to the belief that the God You Are is **separate** from you but somehow connected – **not** One **as** you.

However, mantras and affirmations that **declare the Truth** of Who You Really Are, such as **I AM THAT I AM** have enormous power when spoken with **genuine humility** and the *resolute choice* to BE *Free* NO MATTER WHAT.

Surrender of the *false self* cannot be faked ... the God You Really Are cannot be fooled with insincere haggling for favors to make your separated life more comfortable. You must come **naked, authentic** and **transparent** to the alter of

Your True Self before the shackles of *conditioning* can be exposed for *transformation*.

Self-Discovery will bring up a great deal of **buried anger and rage** that has poisoned and controlled your every thought word and deed. It will strip you of your masks and obliterate your illusions until you are totally **naked** and **empty** and in that emptiness the Truth will enter in all its **Glory** and **Splendor** to show you beyond any doubt whatsoever that ...

YOU ARE GOD

Self-Discovery is **ruthless**, nothing may remain in hiding, none of your coveted and **tasty** cherished *attachments* may be retained, no *expectation* or hoped for outcome may be held as sacred, and absolutely no *identity* that places you outside Who You Really Are may be held back, just in case you one day may need it if God lets you down ... **again**! Yes, **again** ... the *false self* believes that God has betrayed it, let it down in a thousand ways, abandoned it and will continue to do so for as long as it lives ... it must hold something back **just in case** it needs to run and hide or continue to fend for itself. The rug could be pulled from beneath its feet at any moment so it must be vigilant, always looking over its shoulder for any sign of subterfuge or sabotage.

As you come nearer and nearer **absolute Freedom**, the *false self* will act out scenes of **horror and terror** and **viciousness** on the **screen of consciousness** to pull you out of the *Freedom* you have become as **witness** to its dreams in the audience. The *false self* is quite or at least subtle until the stage of dreams is nearly empty and it stands naked before you as the specter of nothing-ness that it is. When this occurs and its reign of terror as the **tyrant** and **jailer** it has been is nearly at an end, it will not hide but seek **to expose** your **worst fears** and **nightmares** in an attempt to keep you imprisoned behind the walls of illusion.

Self-Discovery – Satsang **is** standing in the fire of who you are **not** until the flames burn away everything that is not Real. It is not for the timid who still prefer to live in a **Hollywood spirituality** that seeks to make the *false self's* dream as comfortable as possible - **NO!** The *false self* must be **uncomfortable** in order to be **shaken loose** from the grasp it holds on your *Freedom*.

NO MATTER WHAT

You must have reached *'the point of no return'* where you can no longer endure the **loneliness** and *sorrow*, *frustrations* and *constant fear* in order to reap the meager fruits of the dream world your *false self* calls reality. You must have come to the edge of the cliff, no matter what your circumstances, *attachments*, so called responsibilities and sacred *identities* are and be willing to **chuck it all** for the sake of your Freedom. Jesus said,

"Sell all you have and follow me"

This does not mean you will have to let everything go, it means you must be **willing to** let go of everything if it comes to that – no exceptions! In most cases, in this New Energy, it will not be required to **physically** let go of everything and stand penniless and nearly naked as I was after I made the jump into Self-Discovery. The speed with which *transformation* occurs now is so fast that from one moment to the next you may find that you have stepped over the threshold of dreams and into the audience as a **witness** to the actor you have been and still are, on the stage of illusions … still tethered to the actor but *Free*, knowing that what you are watching is **not** real – not Who You Really Are.

You're longing to return **Home** to Truth must be insatiable. And when it is … you're NO MATTER

WHAT commitment to your *Freedom* will sustain you in the fire of who you are ***not.***

ENERGY FOLLOWS ATTENTION

I have spoken about how important what we give our ***attention*** to is. No matter what we give our ***attention*** to, energy flows into that ***mold*** immediately. You have no doubt heard the old cliché,

"Be careful what you wish for"

This is literally true since focused ***attention*** on anything will eventually bring it into your experience. The catch is and the reason for the warning is that all your *conditioning* ***poisons*** what eventually manifests. You could say that your ***attention*** is filtered through these forgotten and hidden gremlins waiting to show up in what the world often calls – your dreams. By dreams I mean the temporary existence of the dreams or burning desire manifestations you chose to experience.

Once again, let me be perfectly clear, ***You*** as God chose to live in this world of dreams in order to know It/Your Self ... in order to PLAY and for a while in total unawareness of Who It Is – Who You Are. It was not a mistake. The field of dreams has been Its/Your playground and in ignorance of your True and *Only Identity* as *God* you have been able to experience the *deepest darkness* possible. Now, in the New Energy of total Awareness of Who You Are you will consciously experience this field of dreams in the Light of the *Highest Truth*. As I said, the pendulum swings in equal distance from one side of nothing-ness to the other.

Most of humanity's *attention* is placed on temporary things and experiences and in most cases intermittently, meaning not in a consistent enough way to bring what they have been focused on into manifestation. If that had not been the case just imagine how many disastrous things would have appeared. In both of the movie series Pirates of the Caribbean and Narnia the characters experienced the *instant manifestation* of their fearful thoughts appearing as monsters. In the same way, if the three dimensional world humanity has lived within had not been so *slow* to manifest *casual intentions* it would have destroyed the world long ago.

This is *not* the case in the New Energy which is so much faster and this is why the fears that people still cling to in the *imbalanced patriarchy* are manifesting as *chaos* everywhere. From finance to politics to education to war to the media, imbalance is being exposed everywhere and falling like the house of cards it is. The revealing power, accessibility and transparency of our communication systems is no accident, it's one of the instruments of *transformation* the New Energy is using to lift *Global Conscious Awareness* of the Truth in part, by exposing what Truth is *not*.

THE BEGINNING OF SELF DISCOVERY

Discovering who you are *not* is the simplest way to *reveal* the *Truth of Who You Really Are.* There are endless descriptions of *what Truth IS*, *what Reality IS*, *what Love IS* and *Who God IS* and numberless other-worldly states of experience but none touch the *essence* of the God You Are because you cannot place a frame around *infinity*. Words immediately *limit* the Truth, no matter how beautiful they may be. However, words can be effective by *pointing* at what is *not* True – *not* Who You Are.

Mathematics and music, art, photography and film also *point* and are more open ended than words since they do not *tell* you what Truth is, they allow you to interpret through your own *feelings*. I do not speak of emotions, which emanate from the mind of separation, of past memories and hoped for futures, I speak of the *sense* that radiates from the *intuitive* faculty, the telephone line to the Self. It is the instant *knowing* about something that has no frame of reference and *that feeling nature* is where Truth is revealed. It is also where un-truth is exposed as we will see.

I AM THAT I AM

I have found that the most effective and simple way to *expose* what is *not* True within the *false self* is to utter the Truth of Who I AM – Who You Are. This gives attention to the *Truth* which then *Expands*, as does everything we give our *attention* to. For me, the easiest way to say this is,

I AM THAT I AM

This simple way of *declaring* that *You Are God* is an incredibly powerful *trigger* that *opens* the vault of hidden *conditioning* by shedding *LIGHT* on it and *exposing* it. God *IS* Light, not the lightbulb kind of light, although in its capacity as *All That Is*, it certainly *is* that as well. But here I speak of the *radiation* that is unseen by the physical eyes. It is a Light that is also *information* … It *knows* exactly which *conditioning*-gremlin is ready to be exposed … there is no *figuring things out* as there is in the *false self's* linear mind-world. This is what it means when you hear,

'*you need do nothing*'

The Light of the I AM Presence is like a **precise surgical laser beam** that exposes instantly the exact next thing to be *transformed.*

Here is where the **house of mirrors** comes in. Once you have accepted that **everything** in your world is a mirror for what is hiding the **Truth of Who You Really Are** you will recognize the messages and be **Open** to what the Self is sending you. When you are consciously involved in Self-Discovery you will easily become **aware of** and **feel** these messages as the **next** *conditioning*-gremlin to be exposed and have *transformed.*

As I have also said, some mirrors will reveal the incredible **Beauty** of Who You Really Are and this will become your normal experience more and more as the *conditioning*-gremlins are *transformed.* But always, once you realize that none of your *conditioning* defines who you are, you have become the **witness** in the audience **watching the dream** in a state of *Freedom.* This is not **absolute** *Freedom* because you still have *conditioning* that is running but you have distanced yourself far enough away from the dream on the stage to be *witnessing* it **as** the Self … that is living in the Now Moment where the *conditioning* of your past **ceases making a similar future** keeping you in an endless loop of separation and limitation. It **ends the suffering** associated with pain experienced as a victim.

When I first came together with my companion Ingerid, who was a perfectly clear mirror for me, I was literally exposed to a **search-light** beamed directly on my *conditioning*. For me, the first thing to be exposed was my **arrogance**. You might think that walking down a Florida interstate highway in pitch darkness with only the shirt on my back and $5.00 in my pocket, headed towards my aging parents home that I swore I would never do, would have brought me fully **to my knees** in utter humility … and it did. That's when I was ready to move from my knees to my belly.

There is an old saying that,

'you can't trip when you are on your knees'

… it doesn't say you can't be kicked over!

I had made the NO MATTER WHAT commitment to my *Freedom* and that meant **all bets were off** and that **anything goes**. The Self knows this and uses absolutely everything possible to bring us out of hundreds if not thousands of lifetimes of bondage to the tyranny of the *false self* into our absolute *Freedom* in this one lifetime – Now. It may seem **ruthless** but that is often what it takes to break the vice-like grip of the *false self.*

THE PATHLESS-PATH

In this New Energy I choose not to speak of a **path** as most ancient traditions in the 'old energy' did because a path suggests **time** and **space**, which defines the illusion of separation and limitation we are leaving. It places our *Freedom* somewhere out in the future. As I said earlier ONE is ONE … not ONE plus something else and

ONE is always Now

A typical path-seeker will say, *'I am here in the material world,* **working** *towards my Freedom.'* For the *false self* this is music to its ears because it confirms that they have bought into the lie that they are **not Now Free** and as long as this concept is given **attention** it will stay alive and their *Freedom*

... that is the *Awareness* that they are already *Free,* will elude them.

This *simple* Truth is the Alpha and Omega of the New Energy ... everything is Now. Many people speak of this but for most it's *an intellectual concept* and has not yet actually been felt as *Real.* Actually, everyone has at one *time* or another experienced *losing* themselves in something they loved and in that experience losing all sense of time and space and *identity* or person-hood. That experience *was* the Now Moment where separation, limitation, judgment and the *false self* ceased to exist.

The difference was that the experience was *spontaneous* and after it occurred it was little more than a momentary phenomena of some interest. Consciously choosing to Live this way all the *time...* from Moment to Moment feels similar but it is *experienced consciously.* This is the way of manifesting in the New Energy as I will talk about in the next chapter – "The Simplicity of Manifesting in The New Energy."

All attention on *'becoming, working toward, practicing to get better at, procedures to get you there'* and that sort of thing are dropped. Everything speaks of **Being Free Now**. It matters not that the *false self* resists or complains or tells you that you are deluding yourself ... the false self is the master of delusions, or that you are arrogant for saying you are *Free*, what you place your **attention** on **expands**.

In fact, it **is** arrogant to say that you are **not** *Free Now* since God has said that you are. In Psalms and elsewhere in the Bible it says,

"Know you not that you are Gods?"

These kinds of passages have not been given **top billing** on the stage of dreams.

When you say,

I AM THAT I AM

... you are speaking of a **Present Moment Reality** and the God You Are recognizes this Truth and responds accordingly by showing you how your *false self* is attempting to **block** this Truth. Everything in the universe *Now* **comes to your aid** to support the *living experience* of this Truth, despite the *false self's* protests.

You will hear its outraged voice trying every trick it can to persuade you that you are deluding yourself and that it takes years and lifetimes of disciplines and guidance by masters and gurus and formulas and endless workshops and books and videos, and, and, and. And you will most certainly hear protests from other so called seekers if you speak openly about being *Free Now*. Those who have invested years of dedication to the time honored ways and means of the 'old energy' have a vested interest in those efforts being justified as correct. Their protests will be loud and clear … but keep your *attention* on your *Now* Moment *Freedom* just the same.

It does not matter that your *false self* disagrees, its distracting **noise** will fade quickly as you maintain your consistent **attention** on your *Now* Moment *Freedom*. If you **pull the plug** on a laptop it will continue to operate until the reserve power has been depleted. It's the same with your *attention,* there is an echo from past *attention* that the *false self* uses and your mirrors reflect but it **is** limited and will eventually be heard no more. Even the naysayers that once berated you for your arrogant declaration of *Freedom* will dissolve from your life as their vibration cannot resonate with the Light of Truth. They are still God, but sleepers are found in bed not out in the Light *Playing*!

ABUNDANT LIVING

I spent 23 years on the so called *path* while at the same time attempting to find *Freedom* in the 3D world through what it calls success, which included wealth, fame and power and I know from first-hand experience that having achieved all that it claimed was possible – Real *Freedom* cannot be found the way the 'old energy' promotes it.

I am definitely *not* saying Abundance is in anyway a contradiction to Truth, in fact, Abundance *is* another name for God. *All That Is*, which can *lack nothing*, it's another way of saying this. To deny Abundance as the patriarchal experience has taught despite its contradictory promotion of wealth as success, is to express the same arrogance that tells God it is wrong when It says you Are God – You Are *Free - Now*. Abundance includes all aspects of Truth or God – Peace, Freedom, Joy, Beauty, Love and much more … the patriarchal description for wealth as success includes none of these.

On the one hand the spiritual aspect of the **imbalanced masculine patriarchy** has claimed that self-denial and poverty bring you closer to God. The logic was sound because in its **essence** it was speaking again of *attention*. Taking *attention* off the material world made it easier in the slower 'old energy' to keep your focus on God. But this essence was diluted into a **judgment** against Abundant living that survives to this day.

Its day is done though and it's now time to drop this **worn out belief system** – all belief systems in fact. Abundance **is** Who you Are and it is ONE 'as' *Freedom*. It is the **love of** or **attachment** to the energy of money and power and fame that blocks the Awareness of the pristine Beauty, Love and Joy that exists within all facets of the God You Are. When *attachments* and *expectation* of outcomes and all *identities* other than the one identity that YOU ARE GOD are gone, you are *'living IN the world not OF the world'* and that means **Abundant Living**.

FEELING

When you choose *Freedom*, NO MATTER WHAT and are **Open** to all the messages the Self is sending you through the mirror of your life experiences, the blocks or *conditioning* to the Awareness of Who

You Really Are *begin to emerge* and along with that *conditioning, feelings* emerge ... painful feelings. These *feelings* are *at first* the *emotional drama feelings* that emanate from the *mind* and its history of *conditioning* and *later*, once you *move through these feelings* you receive the *intuitive knowing* that *feels* or just *Knows* the *Truth.*

The *emotional feelings* are connected to your *identities, attachments* and *expectation* outcomes and as such are *feelings* *about illusions* despite the very *real-ness* of them.

The *intuitive feelings* or *Knowings* register the *Truth* and arise *after* some form of *conditioning has been felt.* You could say it's the *AHA* after the *OH-NO.*

I remember reading a post from someone quite well known in the spiritual community that I followed due to their global contribution to working with Gaia's shifting energies. She was experiencing some violence in her part of the world and very honestly expressed her concern. The next day she thanked everyone for reaching out to her but also mentioned some people had said they felt it strange that she would express fear being the spiritual world teacher she was supposed to be.

I almost never comment Online unless it's a very brief extension of Love toward something Beautiful but in this case I was literally compelled to send her support and wrote something about how it's natural to experience fear even as a Master when you are still living in a body. The fear in the Master's case is an instinctive reaction and not the same at all as the fear the *false self* has toward the death of its *identity* that taints everything in its experience until it has been *transformed.*

Shortly thereafter I received a reply that shocked me since she was berating me for my comment as if it was an attack on her. I wrote her privately an explanation and said that I had removed the comment so that no one else might misinterpret my support as criticism.

For hours after this incident I felt wretched, not because she had done anything wrong. I was in pain for some other reason that I knew was being **triggered** by this mirror. All my life I had issues with women, strong women as you may have gathered at this point in the book.

My mother's *false self* manifested as very childish in its behaviour but when I was a child she was a God to me, as most children see their parents and this registered as *power* and **strength**. She kept me very dependent on her convincing me that I was physically weak. As a result I was often sick and even lost a year in school due to ill health. This was combined with the *feeling* of being **unseen** and therefore of **no value** ... a conflicting mix of *conditionings*. Although I had no concept of this until I went deep into Self-Discovery every encounter with women throughout my life was an attempt to get my mother to **notice me** and realize that I loved her so I would be **seen**.

It mattered not whether the connection was intimate, at arms-length or very distant and casual such as with the women in this example, the effect of being rejected especially by a strong woman for any reason struck a blow straight to my *false self's conditioned feelings* and this was the mirror I was ready to look at, at the time. Although I had been there several times before during the *transformation* of my *conditioning* it was another and deeper layer I was ready to feel.

Its like driving up the side of a mountain by going around and around, higher and higher. With each revolution you are able to see things you have seen before but from *a **higher perspective*** until you reach the top and everything is visible or *transformed*. At the beginning it can feel disappointing to re-visit some *conditioning* you felt you had already had *transformed* but in Truth it's always at a higher level, although it may not *feel* that way at the time ... in fact it's usually more painful because you have gone deeper into the *conditioning* that has lain hidden for most of your life.

During the few days of feeling wretched I was able to see as the **witness** in a state of *Freedom* the way in which women had been powerful mirrors for the **underlying cause**. This released more *feelings* and more pain in the form of **guilt, shame** and **remorse**, which are at the root of everyone's basic *feeling* of **unworthiness**. Not all mirrored *conditioning* brings up *feelings* that last that long, often it may last only a few minutes, hours at the most but this was a primal issue that was entangled with virtually all my *conditioning* in some way and poisoned my behaviour in ways that often seemed totally unrelated.

It is of great importance to recognize that in order for the *transformation* of any *conditioning* to take place we must ***fully feel*** what comes up when a mirror offers us the opportunity. This is

*'standing in the fire of who you are **not**'*

Nothing about your *conditioning* is Who You Are but to *transform* these blocks you must first expose what is **not** real.

TRIGGERING FEELINGS

Once you dive into Self-Discovery or Self-Inquiry you will often find yourself asking, *'What does this or that mean?*

You could be flipping through a TV Guide and are triggered by a movie that will soon be coming up ... you don't even need to watch the movie that may be days away from viewing to be aware of the **energy** radiating from the movie. It could be a sad romance, a thriller with lots of violence, a documentary about war – anything! It's important to not fall into judgment that spiritual people should not be interested in this or that kind of program. All judgments emanate from the *false self,* including what a spiritual person's **behaviour** should or should not include.

If you find yourself asking the question, *'Why am I interested in this movie?'* then **pay attention** and be **open** to the *feelings* that begin to come up.

For a long while I was drawn to dramas and thrillers where the **bad guy** gets what is coming to him or her. The popularity of these kinds of movies illustrates that the *feelings* they bring up are very common. If for example, you are **ready** to have *conditioning* related to **abuse** be *transformed* then this kind of movie may be a **trigger** for the *feelings* associated with that *conditioning* to come up.

In the past, like me you may have watched the movie and received a **quick-fix** that for a while softened the abuse *feelings* that were surfacing and then forgot about it and went about your life without taking the opportunity to go deeper. The Self is relentless however as I have said and will offer you opportunity after opportunity to *feel* what is ready to be felt and *transformed.*

But finally, when you **do** begin to respond to these triggers, the *feelings* associated with each opportunity will surface. Simply remain **open**, the Self knows what *feelings* and how much you are ready for ... just let these *feelings* flow until they fade whether it be a few minutes, hours or much longer – stay with it.

SAYING YES TO EVERYTHING

What you are doing is saying *Yes* to everything that comes up regardless of how much you may believe that this or that feeling is *not* true, the *feeling* must be allowed to surface and be fully *felt*.

I remember when Ingerid was guiding me through some *conditioning* about my parents that had come up she told me to say that I was *'suppressing feelings of rage and hatred toward my parents'*. I was shocked and resisted very strongly saying this. I told her that *'I may be angry at them for what they did to me as a child but I most definitely did not hate them or feel any rage at all.'*

It doesn't matter if it's not true, it matters that the *false self* **believes** that it's true and that is where the *conditioning* has its origins and for that *conditioning* to be exposed it must be fully *felt*.

Ingerid never paid any attention to what my *false self* complained about, she **knew** these *feelings* were up and running and insisted that I say this.

"I love you too much to treat you like a person" - *Mooji*

When you are in Satsang you *point* to what is *false* and do not allow anyone to *escape* the pain of what is coming up.

*I am not a therapist, but holding Satsang so people can discover by themselves Who they Are, their own Freedom/Liberation when they are allowed to **feel** everything in a safe place, where they are just being pointed at the Truth without continuing to focus on the identification of a broken, not good enough person. - [Ingerid] Esme Ferrer*

It took some time and many more opportunities over a few years before I *got* what she was saying … the depth of its importance, but finally I had a breakthrough and the *AHA* moment of recognizing the *power* of *saying Yes to everything* came upon me.

When we say *no* to any *feeling* that is ready to surface we are resisting the Self's attempt to *Free* us of some *conditioning* and what we resist, which is a form of *attention* … *expands*.

.

The *feeling* may be pressed deeper within and beyond our conscious awareness for the moment but it has grown and *will* emerge somewhere else, louder and more invasive than the last time as a repeating pattern continuing the same suppressed *conditioned* energy. This is why a gentle message from the Self at first may eventually turn into a paralyzing car accident or other life threatening experience when we do not *listen* to *any* of its many messages about what is ready to be *felt* and *transformed*.

The **anger** and **rage** and **hatred** that simmers in the bowels of the *false self's* unconsciousness is like a volcano and *will* find an outlet eventually, be it a heart attack, a stroke, a cancer, some accident or some traumatic life changing experience. In my case thankfully I was sitting on the couch looking at Ingerid's resolute stare and finally saying,

> *'Yes, I 'do' feel these feelings, I 'do' hate my parents'*

... which I finally said and the power of releasing this twisted, ugly, suppressed *feeling* welled up in me like a flood. It was incredibly painful and with it came waves of **shame** and **guilt**.

'How could I be such a terrible person? What kind of monster feels this way about their parents? How can I be God when I feel like this?'

were some of the words I put to these *feelings*.

The poison poured out more and more but finally the flood subsided and with it suppressed *feelings* as well. When this happens there is a **neutral** calm or silence that comes over you like you have squeezed every ounce of this *conditioning* out of its long hidden vault. It now sits there, exposed and **vulnerable** and what you do next is just the opposite of what humanity has done for eons as it rebelled against every kind of *feeling* that did not feel cozy and rosy and happy.

You 'embrace' what came up

Everything is God ... ONE is ONE, there is nothing outside God. Remember I said that God/You went into the dream, **unconscious** of Who It Is so that It could experience in separation and limitation the **deepest darkness** and the **highest Beauty** and **Truth**. It doesn't matter that the dream is an illusion, it matters that it was projected on **the screen of consciousness** in order for God/You to experience It/Your Self fully and when the *conditioning* that resulted from your sojourn into darkness is ready to be *transformed* so that you can again return to full consciousness of your Self *as* God, *embracing **everything*** is the most direct route to your Freedom.

EMBRACING OR FORGIVING?

Embracing everything that comes up is saying ***Yes*** to the moment, to what *is* in the Moment, to the God that everything *Is*. This is the True meaning of Self Love because it says I recognize God *in* and *as* ***everything*** and every ***experience***.

In the 'old energy', a much slower energy where the *false self* could not easily be ***budged*** from its entrenched position as the dictator of your experience, the concept of ***forgiveness*** was effectively used to transform the sicknesses of body and mind that emanated from the self-hatred you felt for living as the *false self* directed you to. Its guidance to look out for yourself in a cruel world of separation and limitation caused you to commit unspeakable horrors upon your self as humanity and with that came buried self-hatred *conditioning* and later the false concept of *sin* and the enormous fear it created for a possible future life of eternal damnation.

The forgiveness of *sins*, which *transforms* self-hatred, initially became an enormous threat to the power the church held over its followers but over time became one of its own most powerful weapons of control.

Forgiveness required that you believe there *is* something to forgive, this much is obvious. Whether you believe there is *sin* or simply *error* it still requires some sort of *transformation*. It traditionally meant an *intermediary* was required who had the *power and purity* to absolve or release people from their sins. The confessional, by whatever label or belief system, became the platform and ultimately became a sort of *bargaining with God* farce where people could do almost anything they desired and have the stain removed if they played the games required of them by the church after the fact. A Course in Miracles says,

'God does not forgive because He [It] never condemned'

This is Truth, God does not condemn It Self for playing a tyrant in a dream It created to know It Self in a state of unconsciousness of *Who It Is*. It does not shoot It Self in the foot any more than it condemns It Self to some hellish existence somewhere/somehow **outside** the Oneness of Its Love. The whole concept is incredibly ridiculous and yet numberless billions have naively bought into it for many hundreds of years.

You may have a very strong vested interest in the concept of forgiveness and if that feels **right** for you then that is your Self's guidance at the moment. It is however much slower than **embracing what is**.

Embracing what is in the moment is **Loving All That Is** ... another name for the God you Are. It does not **first** label something as bad or wrong, which is the language of separation the *false self* uses, it simply accepts that everything no matter how it shows up **Is** God ...every **thing** and every **circumstance**. It recognizes the **Sleeping Beauty** God You/It is who has created much that appears ugly and disgusting, ruthless and cruel within a dream but it doesn't condemn Your/It Self for these experiences.

This does not in any way mean you accept what is imbalanced or turn your back on it if guided to an opportunity to lift the suffering of the world in some way. It means you embrace it all **as** God without the old judgment/forgiveness **two step**.

Forgiveness also has a subtle *arrogance* about it since it tends to place the forgiver in a position of superiority to the one being forgiven as if they have *arrived* at this lofty position of knowing what you have done wrong and chosen to let it go. We are all equal – ALL God.

This *subtle trap* is avoided by simply *embracing* everything – saying *Yes to everything* that shows up. If you really *get* this … its enormous power becomes instantly obvious. You still *act* when you are guided to, to shift circumstances but you don't *buy into* or *identify* with the circumstances as good or bad.

GRACE TRANSFORMS

"Love the Lord your God with all your heart and with all your soul and with all your mind." – Jesus

Self Love *Is* Loving God and in Loving God, *Grace* flows into every situation. I choose to see *Grace* as *Love in action*, the *transforming* power of *Love*. It is always there since It *is* also You *as* God, but without your vulnerable, *open Yes* to *All That Is* it cannot *transform* what is ready to be *transformed*. It's as simple as placing a plug in a socket in order to turn on a lamp, which then illuminates the darkness and removes the false fears associated with what you believed was there.

SUMMARY OF SELF DISCOVERY

-Make the *choice* to be **FREE - NO MATTER WHAT**

-**DECLARE** Who You Are as God by saying **I AM THAT I AM**

-Stay **OPEN** and **LISTEN** for the next *conditioning* that is ready to be *transformed*

-**FEEL** fully everything that comes up … all the anger, rage, shame, guilt, remorse – everything and say *Yes* to all of it, even the feeling to say *No* to any of it, say *Yes* to the *No* as well

-Once the feelings subside, **EMBRACE** everything that came up as aspects of *ALL THAT IS – God*

-After that **GRACE**, *Love in Action* takes over and *transforms* the *conditioning* back into the nothing-ness from which is came

This is the incredible and lightening fast power of *Self-Discovery* that reveals the *Freedom* You Are.

When you have gone through this experience fully *just once* it is impossible to ever see or believe that your *conditioning* defines who you are again. You step off the stage as the puppet of the *false self*, which is nothing more than *conditioning* and into the audience, *Free as* the Self observing as a *witness* the dream-movie being enacted.

You are still tethered to the *false self*-dreamer, but you no longer buy into its lies, its definition of who you are or its control of your experience. This means you are no longer giving it *life* through your *attention*. From this vantage point the blocks to the Awareness of Who You Really Are come up very quickly and the stage player fades into a specter of nothingness leaving the stage empty and in that *emptiness the Truth pours It Self in and absolute Freedom returns*

You will waffle back and forth for a while and go back to *identifying* with the dreamer but the more you **witness from the audience** the more the play on the stage, the movie, the stories and the dramas are seen as **not** you but your puppet who has until now been pulling its own strings.

There is no more **working on yourself** and waiting to be *Free* ... you **are** *Free* instantly when you take your **witness** seat in the audience. From there you realize that you have always been **Free.**

You may call this what you will, there are many, many names for what occurs, I choose to simply call it the *Freedom* that you Know that

YOU ARE GOD

... all doubt-filled intellectual concepts of hope, belief, faith and trust have faded into **Knowing-ness**.

HEALING AND WHOLENESS

When our attention has been drawn inward through physical illness or high stress circumstances we naturally wish to have these issues healed. Healing the body or distressing circumstances gets our full attention particularly when it becomes intense or life-threatening and until we come to the recognition that it is the *Self* speaking to us about our *conditioning*, healing the ***outer condition*** may take our full *attention*. This is always a temporary solution since the *conditioning **will*** find another way to express itself when it's ready to be *transformed.*

Once we take up our position as ***witness*** in the audience, *Free* from the ***suffering*** of ***victim-hood*** all messages, especially the loud ones that manifest as severe physical distress or painful life changing circumstances are recognized as the huge blessings they are.

Nevertheless, as the *conditioning* that brought on these experiences is *transformed* we also wish the experience to be *transformed* but this is not always the case. There can be a number of reasons for this. I used the metaphor of a laptop with the plug pulled still having residual power in the battery and continuing its programs when the power or *attention* has been withdrawn … this is often what prolongs a painful experience for a while after the *conditioning* has been *transformed*. Depending on how much *attention* the *conditioning* received the painful experience may last for some time after the *conditioning* is *transformed.*

However, standing in the Light of Truth or **Being- ness** can also be expressed through the example of pain endured with **Grace.** The radiance of Grace under extreme circumstances inspires many to go within. Nelson Mandela's long imprisonment and the Grace with which he bore the pain and *embraced* his oppressors during and after it ended touched millions of hearts and helped to drive their *attention* inward toward personal *Freedom.*

Your Purpose always includes saying **Yes** to everything, which is the same as *embracing **All That Is*** or **Loving Your Self – God.** Being Consciously Aware of the God You Are is standing in **Wholeness** despite whatever circumstance you may be experiencing.

"Be grateful for the mind whose role it is to molest the false version of yourself until it becomes unbearable and you are left with no choice but to give up and come Home to the Heart"

- Mooji

Chapter Eight

FROM BREAKDOWN
TO BREAKTHROUGH

I have said that living as the *false self and* deeply immersed in the world of separation and limitation, I unknowingly wore a **protective mask of arrogance** to hide my deep fear of being **invisible** and of **no value** to the world or anyone.

I have also explained that this emanated from my relationship with my parents, particularly my mother and that throughout my life I unconsciously attempted to get the *conditioning* my mother represented to **see me** so that I would feel **safe** and **loved**, the Natural feeling you experience when you Know Who You Really Are.

Everything I did was **tainted** by this longing and manifested in many ways, predominately through multiple relationships with women. If a woman showed even the slightest interest in me I clung to that **attention** like it was oxygen to a drowning man.

To **control** these obsessive *feelings* of being noticed, again unconsciously, I needed to somehow tie-down the experiences and marriage was the way the *false self* chose to do this. As a result I was engaged twice without marriage, married four times and had two common-law marriages as well only because I was not yet divorced. I also talked marriage with a number of other women who just looked sideways at me and *never* did I question this behaviour nor did I see myself as *dysfunctional*.

This may be of some value to you if you are ever seeing yourself as a little slow in shifting from the *false self* to the Truth.

Your *false self* can be incredibly *clueless* where its deep *conditioning* is concerned with virtually everyone noticing something is a *little crazy* but you. Some people might even try to be helpful in their own way and say something like,

"But you took the plunge several times ... maybe you should have a look at why you keep doing that!"

And for some time, in my case a very long time, your response might be,

"Hunh, what do you mean?"

I jumped from relationship to relationship, sometimes juggling several in an attempt to *control* my life and smother my immense fear of *invisibility* to somehow make it conform to my *neediness* to be *seen*. And within each relationship there was absolutely *no intimacy* at all … the *masks* I used to appear *above* my *unworthiness* and my deep fear of *abandonment* had me running in circles in an attempt to keep my *personal value safe* and *protected*.

To be intimate with anyone, with life It Self you must be *vulnerable* which represents an extreme form of weakness to the *false self*. In Truth vulnerability is the essence of *power* since it declares openly, *'I have nothing to hide because … of myself I am nothing … no – thing.'* Without intimacy it is impossible to experience *True Joy* because in *Joy* you are *authentic*, and *transparent*, not afraid of exposing anything because you are not *attached* to anything or any special *identity*.

I carried this same tendency into my work in an attempt to control my many *agendas*, needing to know where everything stood and how everyone was thinking and acting … just in case something might fall apart. I hardly had *time to breath*, in fact I was a very shallow breather for many years and remember often hyperventilating when involved in many intense business activities where I was desperately trying to *handle results* and bring about certain *outcomes*.

It is irrelevant that I did eventually so called succeed in business because I was swimming in a swamp of misery every moment until finally I had had enough.

When you have **had enough**, when you have finally reached the stage of saying **I choose Freedom** NO MATTER WHAT, the mirrors **will** show up that you pay *attention* to. For me that was Ingerid and our six years cloistered away quietly, deep in the beautiful and majestic mountains and fiords of Norway.

Ingerid was a perfectly clear mirror for me, **Free** long before I showed up and being exposed to anyone who was still blocked who still resisted the Truth the mirror reflected was an intolerably low and painful energy to endure for any length of time. Consequently, she asked me to leave seven times during the first 5 years. In most cases leaving didn't mean moving down the street it meant going back to Canada or some other country. That alone should have gotten my *attention* but as I said, it took seven departures before my *false self* finally had the **breakdown** that became my **breakthrough**.

The **breakdown** happened when I was staying with an elderly lady in Surrey, UK that I had met at the Heathrow arrivals area seven weeks before. A friend from the Internet had given me a place to stay for a month in London and as we met for the first time at the airport I noticed a jade ring on someone's hand that caught my attention. Jade had always appealed to me and the ring pulled me right over to the lady wearing it. We had a friendly chat for a few minutes and exchanged emails. Later that month we met at the National Gallery in London and after I explained my situation she generously offered me a temporary place to stay while I sorted things out.

Talk about **synchronicity**! That is how God orchestrates our experiences when we are in the flow of Life ... despite my still stubbornly clinging deepest *conditioning*. The back and forth experiences of feeling unceremoniously thrown to the wolves over and over again was **shattering** but that was exactly what was required to *shake* the Real me Free from the shackles of my darkest *conditioning*.

The *false self* interprets such behaviour as incredibly cruel but it took **genuine Unconditional Love** to do what Ingerid did. As long as I have known her she has flowed in Perfect Harmony with the God she Is and that meant pulling my *false self* limb from limb until it **surrendered fully** to the Self.

While on that last exiled experience I found myself alone one cool, misty day in October trudging along a country lane *weeping uncontrollably* for over an hour. I wanted to die the pain was so intense, but die to what? Die to the body? Die to the pain? No! *Die to the illusion* I finally recognized. I could bear the heavy burden of *resistance* to Truth no longer.

When this insight came to me all the relationships I had ever experienced to try and get my mother to *see me* and *love me* and make me *feel safe* came rushing through me like a tsunami. It all made sense *in a flood of insight*. I discussed this with Ingerid through my computer later that day and a week later arrived back in Norway fully *open* and available for whatever I had resisted *feeling* until then.

Over the next few months I went through many painful episodes of *feeling* the *anger* and *rage* I had buried deep within toward my mother *and* father, *but* toward *all* women in general as layer after of layer of this deep *conditioning* peeled away.

As each wave of agonizing pain subsided I *embraced* what had emerged as the God it was and *Grace* - Love in action, *transformed* it back into the nothing-ness from which is came. These calm neutral periods were followed by another and another wave of painful feelings but they came and went quickly because I had said a definitive *Yes* that the Self recognized as *total surrender*. When we arrive at that stage we are Truly *ready* for the

Freedom We Are, the Beauty We Are, the Love We Are to reveal It Self in all its Splendor and Beauty.

STAY DOWN

I used to be like the children's punching bag that bounces right back up when you knock it down. I explained this earlier as my invincibility mask. As an entrepreneur most of my life I had many opportunities to experience this. Nothing could keep me down and I got a lot of welcome **hero** *attention* from this kind of conduct. Little did I know the opportunities I missed by not **staying down** for a while before jumping up and trying again and again.

The collective consciousness of separation teaches this kind of resilient attitude is a sign of courage and determination, but **who** is it teaching?

This helps to **shape** the *conditioning* that makes up our *false self* by telling it what constitutes someone who **fits in** and to the extent that we buy into these stories we blend into a world of mildly miserable unconscious robots that don't rock the boat.

That gloomy day in Surrey while I poured my heart out, I recognized the value of **staying down** for a while when I fell down. Lying there in the mud of so called failure I was able to take an uninterrupted look at myself. And when I looked at what I saw I began to realize that the ideas I had about right and wrong were *made up* by those who had not looked at themselves, not looked within and then passed these concepts on from generation to generation. So I waited in silence, waited to see what might come up if I gave it a chance without any *conditions*. I had said *Yes* to *what is* and it was then that I was Truly ready to discover Who I Really AM.

The discovery was shocking and suddenly my entire world turned upside down, everything I had been taught, everything that had programmed the *conditioning* that defined who I thought I was revealed itself as false and having no reality at all. It was an *emptying* process that lasted for some time and was really scary because being nothing was like being dead but I had shifted my persistence to knowing my *Self* rather than living a lie.

This emptying process was like removing filters from my eyes that allowed me to gradually recognize Who I Really AM and had always been. The revelation was Magnificent, Grand and Glorious - Divine and I realized that everyone was this same nothing-something, nothing-everything that I AM and that *being down* had been an enormous gift I had rejected time and again until I had no choice but to accept it.

Such is the Wonder of the Light that lies at the bottom of despair.

I have said before but it bears repeating often that in the New Energy, where every aspect of life is much faster and the frequency of Truth so predominant it is *not necessary* to go through long and painful years of resisting Truth to finally *breakdown* as I did. You can fall gently into *the loving arms* of your Mother/Father God Self and *surrender* to your feelings right this Moment in the sure and certain Knowing that you will come through the fire of Self-Discovery with *much help* by your side.

Yes, the fire is painful but coming *to* the fire need not be.

Many spiritual practices are pleasant. They don't challenge your identity and its delusion, therefore they are attractive to your mind.

There's nothing threatening when someone tells you, "We're chanting because it purifies the energy and brings you closer to God.

It feels nice for people — adventurous and agreeable. But I'm not interested in adventure, I'm here only for liberation!

Not entertainment for your mind, but the smelling salts that will stun you into awakening.

Mooji

Chapter Nine

THE SIMPLICITY OF MANIFESTING IN THE NEW ENERGY

Once you *shift* into the *audience* as *witness* to the dream-existence of the *false self* you experience a sense of *Freedom* from the *identity* you have believed defined you. These definitions which include your *attachments* and *expectations* of outcomes are now *distanced* from your Self Awareness. As I have said several times, this is not **Total Freedom** as the *conditioning*-definitions are still tethered to you but they can no longer **molest** you in the same way they once did when you believed they represented who you are.

It's as if you have been in a seemingly endless struggle climbing the mountain of **higher consciousness** carrying a backpack filled with rocks. The rocks represent these *identities, attachments* and *expectations* - your *conditioning*. The heavy weight of the backpack continuously captured your *attention* and that *attention* made the backpack heavier and heavier making the top of the mountain seem further and further away and less accessible

When you shift into the audience it allows you the opportunity of *watching* the climber without the heavy weight of the backpack-*conditioning* distracting your *attention* from the top of the mountain which represents Who You Really Are. Your *attention* is only on Who You Really Are and that *attention* **expands** the Truth of It in your Awareness and your experience. Placing your *attention* on Who You Really Are,

I AM THAT I AM

… shifts your Reality.

Now manifesting no longer occurs through the 'old energy' formula that obeys and is tainted by the *false self's conditioning*.

LISTENING

Witnessing the *false self* and it's *conditioning* from the *Freedom* of the audience and keeping your *attention* on Who You Really Are – God, effortlessly brings up whatever is **next ready** to be *transformed*. This is a form of *listening* since you do not need to **do** anything for this **next** *conditioning* to arise … the Self will send you a message and now that you **are** *listening*, it will be easier and easier to recognize. You simply *look* at the *conditioning, feel* it fully, *embrace* it and *Grace* will *transform* it.

As this occurs you will feel lighter and lighter as the rock-*conditioning* is removed from the backpack. You **could** say that they are *transformed* into weightless diamonds that allow the Light of the God you Are to radiate out into your world brighter and brighter.

"If your eye is 'single' you whole body will be full of Light" - Jesus

This passage is paraphrased from the Bible but it is an accurate description of what actually happens. When your *attention* is focused only on the Truth that You Are God *transformation* takes place in your body as well – the very cells of the body vibrate at such a high frequency that they radiate Light to your world and everyone and everything can *feel* this Light … some can actually see it as many great works of art have depicted. Just your **presence** in the world, without saying or doing anything has an **uplifting** influence on everything and every experience.

"A single Liberated being sheds enough Light

to raise the Consciousness of countless beings" –
Mooji

Life does not really begin until you become Aware of Who You Really Are ... until then it's a dream defined by temporary phenomena that come and go. The *false self* requires more and more dazzling phenomena to keep it interested. You see this in the media and in the entertainment industry as wilder and crazier stories, games and shows are splashed across the Internet, newspapers, televisions and movie screens.

I can tell you from first-hand experience that as people still locked in the dream of separation become wealthier their need for bigger and flashier toys and powerful distractions and their addiction to these becomes deeper and deeper imprisoning these so called successful people in a labyrinth of neediness and dependency. In the New Energy world of instant communication, *transparency* allows you to *witness* the authentic from the inauthentic very quickly.

WHAT TO CHOOSE

When you ***know*** Who You Really Are what you hear as you ***listen*** is perfectly aligned with your ***Life***

Purpose. And as you remain *open* to what you hear, whether it's in words or symbols, metaphors or signs, these messages show you *what* exactly to *choose* from the *infinite menu* of creation.

Remember I said earlier that You as God already created *every possibility* and that as God, conscious of Who You Are, incarnated in a physical body with a mind and body that are now in their rightful position as *servants* of the Self, You make *choices* from this infinite menu of creations as you *listen* and are given what *choices* are perfectly aligned with your *Life Purpose*. You don't *think up or imagine* something to create ...

what to choose just comes to you when you listen

Inspirations come to you about *what to do, where to go, what to say and who to say it to.* In the 'old energy' when the *false self* received these inspirations they were always tainted by its *conditioning* and no matter how great the manifestation may have been that eventually appeared in your world, this *conditioning* corrupted the experience with a host of *conditioned*-gremlins that *stole* the natural *Joy* you Are and *Grand* experiences that come 'with' Joy when you are *Free*.

There was a phase in my rise to wealth where I had reached a certain level that would virtually triple my income. There was a waiting period of 90 days before it *kicked in* and I remember how *panicky* I felt while I waited. I felt sick, I slept poorly, I double and triple checked my facts and figures to be sure I followed all the requirements to qualify for the eventual *bump* in my income. I literally *wore* the fear I felt around my whole body like a suit of heavy rusty armor.

Then, when the first check arrived from my lofty new position, I was shaken to the core that the expected *raise* had not occurred. In my anxiety and fear I had indeed made a simple error that erased the giant increase in my income for that month. Although I corrected the error from then on it showed me how debilitating the *fear* associated with my *neediness* could be. I had made a simple error that a high school math student would have picked up because my *false self* was so *attached* to the results that I *expected* that I was blinded to the mistake.

I did not however recognize this *message* from the Self until years later when I began looking at my *conditioning* from the perspective of Self-Discovery so the *conditioning* that caused this *drama* manifested in lots of other ways for many more years diluting and poisoning wonderful New experiences I could have enjoyed fully.

GRATITUDE

When inspirations come to the *false self* it immediately begins planning, complete with lists, timetables and deadlines, imaginative concepts and disciplines. It's an exciting time for the *false self* and it devours the hours and weeks and months as its *dream* begins to take form. It may even be practicing *gratitude* but it's a *contrived* and *control oriented* exercise designed to *make things happen.* The stress emanating from the *false self's conditioning* gets masked in the beginning of a dream project and is scarcely noticed. If it is noticed it is usually regarded as so called *good* stress because the *false self* is having so much fun.

True *gratitude* emanates from the recognition that whatever resonates with your highest *Purpose* is *already done*. When you are *open, listening* to the Self and Aware that it *Is* the Real You – God, you are *listening to* and you are flowing *with* your *Life Purpose*. As with the mind, there is no figuring out anything or trying to make sure it's in everyone's best interest.

Everything you need to know is shown to you perfectly and in the perfect Moment. Everything is aligned perfectly with Who you Are as God, which means it is aligned perfectly with Peace and Love, with Joy and Beauty, with Freedom and Abundance.

'In the hour of your need it is given to you' – Bible

This is **intellectually** known to many but very few live this way as yet, in total **Knowing** that everything you require for your highest Purpose will just **show up** ... you don't need to know the **what, when, why, where, how and who** of it. This does not mean it will just fall from the sky, it may require that you **do** something and that **doing** will be shown to you at the perfect Moment but you won't have to figure it out with the mind as the *false self* believes. Other times people, places, things and/or circumstances **will** just seem to show up, this **is** the **miraculous** way of the New Energy, the way of **Self Mastery.**

SPONTANEITY AND SYNCHRONICITY

Spontaneous moments of synchronicity where everything just comes to together perfectly are part of **being in the moment.** You may have experienced such moments despite still being locked in the world of the *false self*. As I mentioned earlier, everyone has experienced moments of timeless-ness where they were lost in their Joy and the *false self* disappeared in those moments. The dots had not yet been connected to Real *Freedom* and Who You Really Are but a **spontaneous**, **synchronous** moment of living in Truth occurred just the same.

In the mid 1990's I got my first computer and it reminded me that I had a manuscript for a book I had written 8 years earlier sitting in a file cabinet in the basement. This was before the allure of the Internet and all I could think of to use the machine for was record keeping and word processing so I decided to transfer the book to a file on the computer.

It took about 6 months to transpose my scratchy hand written notes, re-write about half the book and change the title several times ... but it was a totally *Joy-filled* experience. The day I finished it I literally heard a voice say,

"So now it's time to get this published!"

I knew nothing about getting published so I went to a book store and as I walked in I was pulled toward a magazine called **'The Sedona Journal of Emergence'** and I picked it up and as I page flipped a section that talked about getting published immediately jumped out at me and grabbed my *attention.* I didn't even read what it said I just went home and called the number.

There must have been a fire drill or something because an editor/publisher never answers the phone of a book publishing company directly, but that day she did. I told her I had written a book and wanted to publish it. She asked what the name was and I said, **'The Millennium Tablets'**. Immediately she said,

"Oh, we might be interested in publishing that!"

I thought,

"Well that's nice"

... not realizing how rare the possibility of this conversation was let alone what she was saying. So she asked me to send her a disc of the book and I would hear from her soon. Three days later she phoned and said,

"Sure, we'll publish this."

... and that was it, easy-peesy-synchron-easy!

Spontaneity and **synchronicity** are expressions of standing in the Awareness of the God you Are, **available** to shift from here to there in a Moment when the Self guides you to ... just **like a little child.** It is also the way **manifestation** shows up in the New Energy.

They appear to function much the same in the 'old energy – success formula' way, but the difference is the **absence of conditioning** attached to all manifestations that the *false self* experiences.

I mentioned that I started a theater promotion company in the early 1980's. I had been working in what my *false self* considered a dreary dead-end job and deeply longing to have a business of my own where I thought at the time my *Freedom* could be found ... and there was the basis of a **burning desire**. Just when my frustration/desire was at a peak I met one of the best known entertainment theater producers in Canada. We hit it off immediately and he told me what Toronto needed was more promotion of groups for its many live theaters.

It wasn't the industry that excited me but that I saw a golden opportunity to start a business of my own in what looked like a well-timed moment. My new friend immediately introduced me to several well placed people in the business but I didn't have the money to start a business. Then, about a week after my first meeting with him, again spontaneously and synchronously I ran into a friend I had helped a few years before when he was virtually living on the street hand to mouth.

He had since then married the daughter of man who owned a large advertising company and started his own ad company occupying an unused building they owned. My friend's company had not worked out but he still had use of this 9,000 square foot, fully equipped building on which he paid no rent. He said, *"Go ahead, just move in and we'll figure it out later once you get started."*

Out of nowhere, like a miracle I was catapulted into my own business. However, all my *conditioned* baggage went with me and 18 months later my business closed its doors but *spontaneity* and *synchronicity* had kicked in because I has listened to the Self's message of *inspiration* in the beginning.

The *creation-choices* the Self sends us are always in *perfect alignment* with our **Life Purpose** and the *fire* that brings about *spontaneity* and *synchronicity* blazes a trail through our experiences. However, without the baggage of the *false self's conditioning* we live in Joy and flow in Harmony with Truth for the good of all.

GRATITUDE

When you are living in the Awareness of the God You Are, you stand in continuous **Gratitude**, knowing that you are being given messages that are in Perfect Harmony with your Highest Purpose. They are not *conditioned* by the *false self* that is trying to make something happen that will reduce its fear masked as success.

You **heard** these inspiration-messages because you were **listening**. Your part, the **individuated God Self** that you Are, living in a body, is to make the **choice** to **receive** these creations. It's a choice you are giving Your Self to experience something New and that something New will always be for the highest good of All ... Pure, Beautiful and Unconditioned.

In Truth however, it is beyond even *receiving*, which is an 'old energy' way that suggests that you will now *get* something that you did not already *have,* that *is not already YOU* and that is another way of expressing separation. You *are All That Is* and lack nothing. You are simply manifesting a physical *extension* of Your Self that has already been created and is ready to be extended into a *manifested expression*.

The enormous power of *Gratitude* is in its Awareness that what you are manifesting already exists *Here* and *Now* and what you give your *Attention* to expands into your experience.

This is totally different than the 'old energy' success formula of manifesting through a *burning desire, a plan, visualization and hard work*. It is effortless even though in some cases it will require you to *do* something but when you are living as your Real Self you are in that timeless, space-less Now where the concept of effort is lost. You could be physically tired, even exhausted afterward but there was no **effort** as your *false self* experiences it.

The core essence of what is manifesting is **You**. There is only You because You are One, you Are God and nothing exists **outside** ONE. The manifestation **Is** you **extended** out into your world which is also entirely You. It is simply a **New** expression, like a unique snowflake of You.

When you come to the place in your Heart where Who You Really Are 'is' your reality you experience your Self 'in' everything 'as' everything that occurs ... separation does not exist, in fact at some point you don't even know what the concept means.

Manifesting from the infinite 'menu' you as God created before time and space, both 'in' your Self and 'as' your Self is simply a matter of choice. Even the concept of deciding what to choose simply comes to you and is always in Perfect Harmony with your Joy, which is also Who you Are.

'Everything 'is' God and is felt 'as'

Love, Abundance, Joy, Peace, Freedom and Beauty.

Its ALL 'inside You

There is no separation no matter how God shows up, the disguises that have masked this Truth have all fallen away

THE CREATIVE CHOICE

I have mentioned a few times that as One, God is always Now and therefore the concept of creating something that does not Now exists is not possible … everything that can possibly *manifest* as a *thing* or an *experience* has already been created and we, as God, consciously or unconsciously choose from an *infinite menu* of already created possibilities.

We receive the perfect choices for our Highest Purpose all the time as *inspirations* which the *false self* believes is an expression of its creativity but the Self Knows it is an aspect of It Self ready to come into the world of time and space and be experienced multi-dimensionally without conditioning.

When a musician receives the music and lyrics for a song he or she is *downloading* an already complete musical creation in snippets. They will get a bar or two, then another and another until the piece of music arrives completely. Then, lyrics will arrive or the download may come in the reverse or even pieced together one verse at a time.

Mozart was known to receive an entire symphony *in a flash* and then write down the notes to it like dictation without a single correction. This is the multi-dimensional way of choosing from the infinite menu of creation ... from one dimension complete in every way to another dimension where it can be *savored* and *tasted*. Until now, for most people it has been in tiny jigsaw pieces but as humanity transforms back into the Awareness of Who It Is as God, the experience will be more like the Mozart way ... spontaneous and synchronistic.

Everything IS God and as we become Aware of the Truth of this there is a *fluidity*, a seamlessness about the creative experience that is unknown to the *false self* but which reveals more and more expressions of the infinite and boundless ONE that we Are.

SUMMARY OF THE SIMPLICITY OF MANIFESTATION

-Stay **Open** *and* **LISTEN** for the *inspirations* of the Self of what creations to *choose* as aspects of your *Life Purpose*

-**CHOOSE** what the Self has shown you

-Express **GRATITUDE** often that it is *already done*. Do not try to figure out any of the details, the **God** You Are *extends* It Self into those *manifestations*, the *when* and the *how* requires *no attention.* You simply fall into the *Unknown* and *Know* that everything is already taken care of.

*"What the Universe - the God You Are will **manifest** when you are in alignment with It is a lot more interesting than what you - the false self tries to manifest" – Adyashanti*

If you need to *act* you will be shown. If you need *do nothing* you will be shown.

DON'T LIMIT THE GOD YOU ARE

What you are doing when you stay *Open* and say *Yes* to everything from the position of *witness* is to be *empty*, which is the Truth about Who You Really Are in the un-manifested state.

You are not telling the God You Are *what* is best for you … that comes from the *conditioned false self.* You are a *blank screen* that says,

Tell me where to go, what to do, what to say and to whom and what I need to know for my highest Purpose.

It is falling empty handed into the loving arms of your God Self knowing that all is well and whatever you are guided to do or **not** do will be for your highest good, your highest Purpose.

In this way you are not limiting the God You Are and your life experience will unfold Abundantly in all its Glory and Grandeur and Love.

Be empty, that's it!

When you are empty you are the most powerful

Because you are Present.

You are Awake. You are Alive.

And you are nothing,

- Mooji

Chapter Ten
ABUNDANT LIVING

SELF Mastery 'is' Abundant Living. You do not 'live' life, you 'are' Life and It 'Lives' You

In an earlier chapter I quoted a line from in A Course in Miracles and it's appropriate to repeat it here:

Nothing Real can be threatened.

Nothing *un-Real Exists.

What can be threatened, that is … what has a beginning and an eventual end? This is an easy question and covers every manifested thing or experience there is, ever was or ever could be.

You as God *extend* an expression of your Self into a temporary shell called a thing, be it person, animal, vegetable, mineral, sub-atomic particle or any experience no matter how small or grand, all still *contained* within your Self. Then you step into them and play with them until the moment comes when they dissolve back into You as no-thing – emptiness.

What a wonderful concept!

But for a brief moment, eons of time to the *false self*, you do this **unconscious** of the God you Are and this swings the pendulum as far as it can in the direction of **imbalance and chaos**. Then you remember Who you Are as God, as humanity is Now doing and the pendulum swings in the other direction just as far. Then, at some point you *rest* into nothing-ness or *emptiness* in the center. This emptiness is your natural state and can be experienced at any moment when you are Aware of Who You Really Are as God.

EVERYTHING IS INSIDE 'ONE'

Everything and every experience *is* You, made *out of* You, *as* You and experienced *by* You.

When you experience Life in this way you have returned to the Awareness that you Are God, and you Know that You *are* the **Master** of the Life that You Are ... how could you not be?

The *dream-manifestation* that the world, the universe, the multi-verse were created to *play* in and *know* Your Self in has returned to your Awareness.

The *seriousness* that is wrapped around so much of spirituality is gone and you *know* what it means to *be* a child again ... not *childish* as the *false self* is but innocent, light and playful.

You deny your Self nothing, you fully *savor* everything, you enjoy everything *as* your Self. There is *no fear* that your *living expressions* will *wound* or *damage* or *contaminate* your world because when you are Aware that you Are God, *nothing* you experience is *out of balance*, nor does it contradict the *Love You Are* and have for Your Self.

This is why when you live in Conscious Awareness *as* the **God** you Are, as the *Master* you Are, *it is impossible to introduce discord into anything*, to bring competition, attack, defensiveness, war, imbalance or any concept your *false self* has expressed as a result of its *conditioning* to any other extension of Your manifested Self. Everything you do, every expression you extend *from* your Self *to* your Self is an expression of *Love for* your Self and it can be *felt* by all living things and all experiences ... and all things and experiences *are* living.

In this Awareness of Who You Are you are no longer *dazzled* with phenomena you know that *all* phenomena is a temporary expression of Your Self. It could be fireworks, a roller coaster ride, an intoxicating spring fragrance or even a moment of Bliss, they are *all* temporary and therefore not **real*. Yes, *you savor and enjoy* them fully but you are not in any way *attached to* or *controlled by* the temporary nature of any phenomena. You enjoy the *show* as you rest in the Peace that You Are in the Knowingness that you Are *All That Is*, in whatever way you show up.

THE MASQUARADE

Now you attend the Masquerade Ball playing any part you choose but not *lost* in the part as some actors find themselves after continuously playing the same character onstage for months and years. The *false self is* that actor, lost in the ever changing character it is playing as it wears mask after mask.

The Self that is fully Aware of Who they Are may *still wear masks* from time to time but consciously and as a game or, you may *walk unnoticed* throughout the world radiating the Peace and Joy and Love that you Are in total silence. Any and every possibility is open to you.

I lived in the UK in the mid 1980's just as I was beginning the years of building the wealth I experienced and late one foggy evening I was standing alone in a combination train/tube station a little ways out of London waiting for a subway car to take me home. I was desolate after an unsuccessful meeting with an executive I had contacted from Canada who I was certain would join me in my business ... in fact his initial long distance enthusiasm about what I was offering was part of the reason I had decided to move across the Atlantic.

I had waited in the damp cold for about thirty minutes feeling more and more depressed when an elegant and elderly man about 5 feet tall, dressed in an expensive looking topcoat, a bowler hat and carrying a walking stick suddenly stepped out of the darkness, smiled warmly and exclaimed with an powerful tone of authority,

"You look like someone who knows what he is doing, do you know when the next train to Waterloo station arrives?"

Well ... I couldn't have been more shocked out of my despair if I had been hit by a bolt of lightning. I shifted immediately from dark and gloomy to pride-filled that I was ***seen*** in this way. It was a swift and powerful stroke to my *false self's* **in the dumps** mood but it pulled me right up out of this darkness and into the Light. As I said before the building up of the collective *false self* from the **unworthiness** and **less than** consciousness it has been in for thousands of years is a precursor for many people to becoming Aware of their Natural Worthiness as the God They Are.

As it turned out I had no idea when any train or subway car would arrive as the lightbulb over the train/tube schedule was burned out. Then the ***surreal little fellow*** who had instantly helped to shift me from dark to Light smiled warmly, nodded his thanks and descended the steps from the tube platform to the train platform a short distance below. I watched him with a cheerful grin on his face descend the only steps available to the train platform below.

As I stood shivering for another half hour waiting for a subway car I was ***lost in the glow*** of this momentary meeting and scarcely noticed that it had been over an hour since I arrived at the station. Then I realized, even this late in the evening that a subway car should have arrived by now. My first thought was for the little fellow waiting on the platform below since no train had arrived either or I would have definitely heard it, so I felt I should go have a look and see how he was.

I descended the few steps to the train platform but when I arrived at the bottom he was nowhere to be seen. I immediately panicked thinking he must have fallen over the side to the tracks below but I thought that was not likely as I would have heard the sound of a body hitting the ground and tracks below since the station was very open and I was close enough to hear the noise. Nevertheless, now distraught I ran up and down the landing peering over the side which was well lit to see if he was lying injured below, but nothing ... he was nowhere to be seen. Also, there were no stairs that led down to the tracks and it was too steep for the little fellow to have jumped for whatever reason. I knew he had not come back up the stairs because I had been standing right beside them. He had simply vanished!

You may make of this story whatever you will but for me this event stayed with me and touched my heart many times over the years in the same way as the man on the streetcar when I was a teenager. Whenever I was feeling *low, unworthy or downcast*, which was a lot recalling this incident could instantly brighten my spirits. Whether he was some lofty spiritual entity or just a man, in that moment he was a Master mirror for Who I Really AM and the influence was life changing.

Later the influence of these *two magical encounters* shifted from the *false self's conditioning* to the Self as a mirror. I feel that both these experiences were *Grace* or *Love* in action and examples of what a *Master* can and does extend to their world whenever the Perfect Moment arises.

This is the mighty influence you have everywhere when you are standing in your *True Power* as the individuated God-Self You Are. And that Light of Truth is continually mirrored back to you in every moment.

This is *Abundant Living*

Whether you require *untold wealth* to manifest in your life to extend your Life Purpose to the world or the *absolute basics* of food, shelter and clothing, nothing that you require to live your True Purpose will be missing at the exact moment you require it. In either case, when you stand in your True Power every Moment is a reflection of the Beauty, the Abundance, the Love, the Joy, the Peace and the Freedom that you Are as God.

*It is important to understand that as we **shift fully** into the New Energy, that God - US, is embodying It Self fully into the **material world** - fully conscious of It Self. We are no longer trying to **bliss** ourselves out of it to return Home as spirituality often taught in the 'old energy' ... we are embodying Home or Heaven **in** this physical world as well as in all other dimensions. This is the meaning of bringing Heaven to Earth.*

*What is 'un-Real' does emanate from a temporary extension of You to You – God to God and as such there is a 'real-ness' to it. This is a Divine Dichotomy and cannot be explained.

*"The **Self** is not to be found as a prize at the end of a long journey. It is not produced or created. It is, in fact, a **discovery**, a **recognition**"*
– Mooji

Chapter Eleven

IT'S TIME TO SHINE

"You only have to keep choosing Truth.

– Mooji

Each of us has a *Life Purpose* chosen by us before we entered this incarnation and that Purpose becomes crystal clear when you take your seat of Power, Aware of Who You Really Are.

Everyone who has this Awareness just by *Being* becomes a Bright Light that automatically radiates the Truth into the world and humanity and each *New Light* makes it easier and easier for humanity to also rise into this Awareness. You could call this the *foundation* of everyone's *True Life Purpose*. Everywhere you hear about people trying to *change* the world but Real change occurs when you become *consciously Aware* of Who You Really Are. When this happens you literally *are* Your True Self embodied *as* Heaven. There is one planet but over 7 billion worlds ... and for you, it *is* Heaven on Earth.

When you *manifest* Who you Really Are in a physical body,

It's Time To Shine

Once again there is no figuring out *what* you should do, if there is *a doing* beyond just *Being the Light that You Are*, you will be shown. Whether it be a global influence of some sort or something that appears to be on a smaller scale, everything extended *from* God *to* God is part *of* God's *perfection* and blends into the perfect Wholeness that It Is.

This is what is occurring throughout humanity as hundreds of millions of souls are not only *awakening* from eons of slumber in the world of separation and limitation but are *shifting* from that position of *potential Freedom* to the actual experience *of Freedom* as they discover Who they Really Are. Many are still working with 'old energy' ways and means, which as I have said several times is a much slower way to *Freedom* but if their *Joy* lies there then for them, that *is* the way for them at the moment.

Others, who have sensed that *Freedom* is here Now will settle for nothing less NO MATTER WHAT and choose *timelessness* as their pathless-path Home - Now.

THE VISION

Just as each snowflake is unique so is the manifestation of *Purpose*. For Ingerid' Esme Ferrer Enzo, the Master I lived with for 7 years in Norway, **THE VISION** as she calls it is that unique snowflake. It was given to Ingerid many years ago in a flash of insight..

I spoke earlier about the foundation of your *conditioning* being **unworthiness** and how it occurred as a result of your separation from the conscious awareness of Who You Really Are. I said that this manifested in a number of ways including *poverty consciousness* which still pervades the collective consciousness of humanity to this day.

Religion has twisted the concept of poverty into a virtue while portraying itself as a grandiose reflection of Abundance, the sole mediator between God and man. The opulent structures it has erected all over the world stand in stark contrast to the often destitute circumstances of its followers who have blindly followed its **imbalanced version** of austerity, temperance, moderation, self - restraint and self-denial.

The imbalance of this teaching has reached its end and the New Energy will reflect in every way the Abundance each of us *is*. Here in Ingerid's words is,

BEAU MONDE - THE VISION

"The Vision was given to me during the last decade.

*THE VISION will be **acts of celebration** of human genius, creativity, compassion, and innovation. Together we can fulfill our deepest Heart's desire for Peace, Love and Oneness and to give our unique gifts for the good of the whole. For me this is a Love Affair that will never go away.*

IT is the True expression of Divine Freedom and Wildness, the True Fire of Creation and we want everybody to hear the roar that silently encourages others to live wildly, free and authentic. Our permission to do so has been granted as it is our Divine Birth-right. We are all in this together and we are on Fire. We all know the necessity of World Peace and the Birth-right of Human Dignity.

This is the Birth of a Dream, a Symphony of Soulful Messages and an Instrument for True Intelligent Life, a level where you have no other choice than to Live from your Heart and Intuition in the Now

Moment, born to express your Gratitude to Life It Self and The Birth of a New World, a New Era.

*We are Open to Sacred Emptiness, Eternal Mother flowing effortlessly and expressed limitlessly through our Natural Divine **creativity, playfulness** and **spontaneity**, extending True Freedom, Love and Joy and supporting this Beautiful Time of Awakening Humanity in Beautiful decorated **Galleries** where the Silence speaks through **Satsang**.*

*They will be **safe places** where the Beauty of Truth and the Power of Unconditional Love, Absolute Freedom and Total Openness embody Wilder Grace, the Emerging Power of the Divine Feminine and Divine Masculine."*

*For me **THE VISION** expresses and represents the **Absolute Truth**,*

YOU ARE GOD

The New Energy **ends** the concept of a separate identity or personhood and shifts to the Natural identification,

I AM
ALL THAT IS

Ever since Ingerid revealed the *Grandeur* of it to me it has filled me with Passion and a Fiery longing to extend the Love I AM to the world and humanity.

When you are fully Aware that you *Are* God all sense of a separate self with its many *attachments* and *expectations* has been *transformed* and to *play* in the field of temporary manifested things and experiences is a *completely natural* and *Joy-filled* experience unencumbered by any sense of loss when it returns into the emptiness from which it sprang.

Anyone who experiences a *Gallery* will feel the natural Silence, Peace, Serenity and Simplicity that lives *within Abundance* and is a Perfect reflection of Who They Really Are and that what they give their *Attention* to will *expand*. In this way the Truth that

YOU ARE GOD

will be constantly expressed in exquisite physical manifestations.

Whatever comes, let it come; what stays, let it stay; whatever goes, let it go.

—*Papaji*

EPILOGUE

When you come to the Awareness of Who You Really Are, *Free* from all tethering to the *conditioning* of the *false self* you begin to Truly Live your **Life Purpose**. There is no need to look for It, It will just be felt and Known as Why you are here *as* God in a physical body.

There will be no agendas, control, stress or have-to's about your Purpose It will simply flow effortlessly without *attachments* or *expectations from* You and *as* you.

You will walk through your Life experience as Peace, Joy, Abundance, Freedom, Love and Beauty radiating these beams of Light from the God You Are without the need to do anything. If there is a doing of any kind, it will be **timeless** and **boundless** and flow easily in the midst of any chaos that still remains on the planet.

Here is what Ingerid has to say about this experience that she Knows and lives:

*When an Enlightened one offers Self Discovery Satsang that one can never **not** see the other person, they are the only ones who Truly **do see** another.*

Before you are Totally Free fear sends out energy that people pick up and makes them feel the opposite of what you want them to feel which is Eternity and Peace. It is the fear that one will not be able to handle all kinds of people's expectations, stresses, moods, anger and hostile energies.

*Whatever meetings with others that may occur just let them unfold standing in your I AM Presence and when required you will have no difficulty telling them that they must come back when they are **more ready**.*

It is not your responsibility to make them safe or get what they paid for or be responsibility to fill them up with spiritual phenomena. You must always hold them fully responsible for their own so called process.

Freedom is not a spiritual phenomenon, it is their nature, and saying Yes to that is raw ... it collapses all the old conditioning.

I do not recognize your false self or give it any attention ...we are Love Itself, which is Total Freedom, Life Itself with no limitations and no definitions.

A Multi-millionaire until 1999 John traveled for decades around the world speaking to tens of thousands of people before leaving everything behind and diving into Self-Discovery. Now, in the first baby steps of The Golden Age, John shares his acquired understanding of the 'old energy' of the *mind* together with his personal experience of The New Energy - *Thinking with the Heart*, which is the instrument of SELF Mastery, Abundant Living and Freedom - Now

Website

johnmcintosh.info

Testimonials

"John is one of the bravest men I know because he is not afraid of stepping out of thousands of years of

old imbalanced masculine, patriarchal power and belief systems which is necessary to reveal the true Divinity of a real and authentic man. He is not afraid of being open and vulnerable, knowing that is True Power and what the world needs in this Time of profound and dramatic Change. "- Ingerid Esme Ferrer, CEO World Galleries of Esme Ferrer Beau Monde.

John ... I loved this book immensely. Your openness to share your vulnerabilities was most heart warming and I applaud your commitment to share your hard earned lessons of the ascension process. Finbar Tallon

"Your 'words' resonate very deeply" - Bjørg Landro

1000 people can say something and you hear Nothing but then ONE [says] IT and YOU GET IT, it touches Deeply! Gratitude just doesn't seem adequate. - Dee Marlowe

"Thank you John, your writings are translucent drops of divine nectar...that when dropped from eye to mind to tongue to heart invoke a subtle harmonic alchemy that allows love to sing a most hypnotic

melody, lifting the veil, and opening the portal to Presence" - Pamela Jane Gerrand

"Thank you John for the credible clarity you provide and the direction you offer us ALL as we unravel our way into Home" - Joie Bourisseau

"John's books and teachings have transformed my life and opened up my soul to incredible heights. His guidance and wisdom have not only brought me material success, but best of all spiritual riches that I have searched for my entire life. Not only has he inspired me, he has helped me find truth and focus from where I needed it most – 'inside of me'. Thank you John." - Chris Carley – (number #1 company distributor) - Herbalife International